Lecture Notes in Computer Science   1658
Edited by G. Goos, J. Hartmanis and J. van Leeuwen

Springer
*Berlin
Heidelberg
New York
Barcelona
Hong Kong
London
Milan
Paris
Singapore
Tokyo*

Joachim Baumann

Mobile Agents: Control Algorithms

 Springer

Series Editors

Gerhard Goos, Karlsruhe University, Germany
Juris Hartmanis, Cornell University, NY, USA
Jan van Leeuwen, Utrecht University, The Netherlands

Author

Joachim Baumann
Asternweg 8, 71106 Magstadt, Germany
E-mail: joachim.baumann@epost.de

Cataloging-in-Publication Data applied for

Die Deutsche Bibliothek - CIP-Einheitsaufnahme

Baumann, Joachim:
Mobile agents : control algorithms / Joachim Baumann. - Berlin ;
Heidelberg ; New York ; Barcelona ; Hong Kong ; London ; Milan ;
Paris ; Singapore ; Tokyo : Springer, 2000
  (Lecture notes in computer science ; Vol. 1658)
  ISBN 3-540-41192-5

CR Subject Classification (1998): C.2, I.2.11, D.1.3, D.2, D.4.4-7, K.6.5

ISSN 0302-9743
ISBN 3-540-41192-5 Springer-Verlag Berlin Heidelberg New York

This work is subject to copyright. All rights are reserved, whether the whole or part of the material is concerned, specifically the rights of translation, reprinting, re-use of illustrations, recitation, broadcasting, reproduction on microfilms or in any other way, and storage in data banks. Duplication of this publication or parts thereof is permitted only under the provisions of the German Copyright Law of September 9, 1965, in its current version, and permission for use must always be obtained from Springer-Verlag. Violations are liable for prosecution under the German Copyright Law.

Springer-Verlag Berlin Heidelberg New York
a member of BertelsmannSpringer Science+Business Media GmbH
© Springer-Verlag Berlin Heidelberg 2000
Printed in Germany

Typesetting: Camera-ready by author
Printed on acid-free paper   SPIN: 10704127   06/3142   5 4 3 2 1 0

Foreword

Order out of chaos can be the motto of many sciences, and the research on mobile agents is no different. Mobile agents are inherently chaotic entities that we all attempt to tame. Over the last 5 years, mobility has been one of the most thoroughly researched topics of the agent field. As the technology has evolved and matured, research on mobility is now focusing on subtopics crucial to the long-term success of mobile agents.

In this book on the topic Joachim Baumann provides in-depth coverage of essential research issues, namely mechanisms for locating and terminating mobile agents, and for orphan detection in a mobile agent system. Through this book, you will gain insights into the design and implementation of three control mechanisms for use in mobile agent systems: the energy concept, the path concept, and the shadow concept. J. Baumann examines these mechanisms and offers a solid argument as to why they would be better choices over existing mechanisms with respect to message complexity, migration delay, and availability.

J. Baumann has done an outstanding job in advancing the science of mobile agents. This book helps us better understand how to *tame* mobile agents. I hope you will find the information of as much value as I have.

June 2000   Danny B. Lange
Chief Technology Officer
General Magic, Inc.

THE ROAD NOT TAKEN
Two roads diverged in a yellow wood,
And sorry I could not travel both
And be one traveler, long I stood
And looked down one as far as I could
To where it bent in the undergrowth;
Then took the other, as just as fair,
And having perhaps the better claim,
Because it was grassy and wanted wear;
Though as for that the passing there
Had worn them really about the same,
And both that morning equally lay
In leaves no step had trodden black.
Oh, I kept the first for another day!
Yet knowing how way leads on to way,
I doubted if I should ever come back.
I shall be telling this with a sigh
Somewhere ages and ages hence:
Two roads diverged in a wood, and I -
I took the one less traveled by,
And that has made all the difference.

Robert Frost

Preface

A comparatively new paradigm in the area of distributed systems is the mobile agent paradigm. Mobile agents promise to deal very efficiently and elegantly with dynamic, heterogeneous, and open environments as e.g. the Internet.

A mobile agent is an active entity that can act on behalf of its user, following a given task. The agent can autonomously migrate through the network during its execution. While it computes, it is able to observe its environment and to adapt dynamically to changes. It can continue its computations asynchronously even if the user that has started it, is (temporarily) not connected to the network. By moving the agent to the host on which data resides, communication latency and bandwidth consumption may be reduced in many cases.

Applications for mobile agents are widespread and encompass not only applications in electronic commerce environments and applications to search and filter global information spaces, but can also be found in the areas of network management, monitoring, information dissemination, or parallel processing. These are only some of the application areas on which many different authors agree. In all of these applications mechanisms are needed that provide the user with the ability to control mobile agents.

In this book several control mechanisms for mobile agents are presented, i.e. mechanisms for locating and for terminating mobile agents, and mechanisms for orphan detection in a mobile agent system.

First, control mechanisms are discussed that have been specifically designed for mobile agent systems, taking into account the peculiarities of the mobile agent paradigm. The energy concept is presented, which supports orphan detection for mobile agents. In this concept every agent gets some energy. Every action the agent takes, every service that is used, costs energy. When the energy is used up, the agent is terminated. Then the path concept will be discussed, a variant of which is used in the area of distributed systems to track mobile objects. Every agent leaves a path in the system, i.e. on migration, information is left behind about the agent's target place. This path can be followed to find the agent, and/or to terminate it. The third concept presented is the shadow concept. This concept supports locating and terminating of mobile agents and furthermore, provides orphan detection for mobile agent systems. This concept combines the energy and the path concept in a way that leaves the agents most of their autonomy, has low communication costs, and provides excellent fault tolerance (i.e. a high availability). An agent leaves a trail in the system, but in contrast to the trail in the path concept, this trail is cut short in regular intervals. To allow for simple termination of agents, a delegate of the application is left in the system, the shadow. As long as the shadow exists, all dependent agents are allowed to continue their work. The agents are no longer depending on the availability of the application. Thus no permanent connection between agents and application is needed, an application can e.g. run only intermittently to check for results. Furthermore, we discuss for each of these concepts fault tolerance and message complexity.

In the area of distributed algorithms, mechanisms have been developed to solve similar problems (i.e. termination detection and distributed garbage collection). Using a transformation, an algorithm of one class can be changed into an algorithm of the other class and vice versa. In fact, new algorithms were discovered this way.

A similar transformation providing the conversion of either of these classes into control algorithms for mobile agents should allow access to a large number of algorithms for controlling mobile agents. But the failure model of the area of distributed algorithms and that of the area of mobile agents are radically different, ruling out the direct use of these mechanisms.

Instead we will use transformed garbage collection algorithms to show the following: all the principles of the transformed algorithms can be found in the control mechanisms developed explicitly for mobile agents. Furthermore, if a new, radically different algorithm is developed either in the area of termination detection or in the area of distributed garbage collection, it can be transformed at once and its principles can be exploited for developing new control mechanisms.

Finally, the control mechanisms are compared with mechanisms presented in the literature regarding reliability, message complexity, interference with the agent autonomy, and usability for applications.

This book is an extended version of my PhD thesis, and a large number of people helped in creating both the thesis and the book; without them it would not have been possible to realize them. First of all I have to thank Prof. Kurt Rothermel and Prof. Friedemann Mattern for their help. Both were ever willing to motivate me anew, and to point me to new directions of importance for my work.

I would like to thank many colleagues at the IVPR for suggestions and advice. Most of all I have to thank my colleagues and friends of the Mole project for their constant help. The discussions with Fritz Hohl, Markus Straßer, and Markus Schwehm were very important for this work, as were their comments regarding this document. Furthermore, I have to sing their praise regarding their fine and never-failing sense of humour, and for the ability to point out the good in every situation.

And I have to thank all those students who, in implementing the Mole system and the protocols, were crucial for my work to succeed. Especially important to me are those of the students who became more than part-time colleagues. These friends are: Bernhard Beck, Jens Höfflinger, Michael Paulus, and Matthias Zepf. I have to thank Felix Gärtner from the University of Darmstadt for his helpful comments regarding fault tolerance.

Then there is my family: I have to thank all of them, my mother for teaching me the important things in life, and for believing in me, my parents-in-law for readily welcoming me in their family, for their good-natured humour, and their always ready willingness to feed me (there is nothing better than their Fleischkäsrouladen[1] and Spätzle[2]), and my wife, Annette, for her support and for cheering me up.

Finally I have to thank Prof. John Argyris, for starting it all.

I do not regret that I took this road.

June 2000 — Joachim Baumann

---

1. You take thin slices of Fleischkäse (a meat loaf made of ham and pork or veal) and roll it, filling the roll with cheese, small cucumbers and mustard. Then you put it in the oven for half an hour, together with a sauce of tomatoes and sliced onions.
2. Spätzle are swabian noodles, infinitely better than all the italian cuisine has to offer (at least in my opinion).

Table of Contents

1 **Introduction** 1
2 **Mobile Agents** 5
   2.1 Introduction to Mobile Agents 6
      2.1.1 A Short History of Mobile Agents 6
      2.1.2 Properties of Mobile Agents 7
      2.1.3 Applications 8
   2.2 Examples of Mobile Agent Systems 9
      2.2.1 High-Level Language-Based Systems 10
      2.2.2 Language-Independent Systems 12
      2.2.3 Standardization Efforts 14
   2.3 Our Agent Model 14
      2.3.1 Relations between Agents 15
   2.4 Control Mechanisms for Mobile Agents 17
   2.5 Related Work in the Area of Mobile Agents 18
      2.5.1 Locating Agents 18
      2.5.2 Orphan Detection 20
      2.5.3 Termination 21
3 **System and Failure Model** 23
   3.1 Our System Model 23
   3.2 Our Failure Model 23
4 **Control Mechanisms for Mobile Agents** 25
   4.1 The Energy Concept 26
      4.1.1 The Idea 26
      4.1.2 The Protocol 27
      4.1.3 Discussion 29
   4.2 The Path Concept 29
      4.2.1 The Idea 30
      4.2.2 The Protocol 30
      4.2.3 Discussion 33
   4.3 The Shadow Protocol 33
      4.3.1 The Basic Protocol 33
      4.3.2 Hierarchical Shadows 41
      4.3.3 Mobile Shadows 49
      4.3.4 Strategies for Moving the Shadows 58
      4.3.5 Possible Optimizations 60
      4.3.6 Comparing the Path Availabilities 61
      4.3.7 Discussion 64

5 Distributed Garbage Collection 65
5.1 System and Failure Models 66
5.2 Introduction to Distributed Garbage Collection 66
    5.2.1 A Computation Model for Distributed Objects 67
5.3 Reference Counting Schemes 68
    5.3.1 Direct Reference Counting Algorithms 68
    5.3.2 Weighted Reference Counting 73
    5.3.3 Local Reference Counting 76

6 From Garbage Collection to Control Mechanisms for Mobile Agents 79
6.1 A Computation Model for Mobile Agents 80
6.2 Agents as Parent Objects 81
    6.2.1 The Idea 81
    6.2.2 Simple Reference Counting 81
    6.2.3 The Variant of Lermen and Maurer 83
    6.2.4 The 3-Message Variant of Rudalics 86
    6.2.5 The 4-Message Variant of Rudalics 88
    6.2.6 Weighted Reference Counting 88
    6.2.7 Local Reference Counting 89
6.3 Dependency Objects as Parent Objects 91
    6.3.1 The Idea 91
    6.3.2 Direct Reference Counting 92
    6.3.3 Local Reference Counting 94
6.4 Assessing the Transformations 96
    6.4.1 Agents as Parent Objects 96
    6.4.2 Dependency Objects as Parent Objects 98
6.5 Combining the Transformations 99
    6.5.1 Local Reference Counting plus Weighted Reference Counting ..100
6.6 Discussion 101

7 Comparing the Mechanisms 103
7.1 Functional Comparison 103
7.2 Categorizing the Mechanisms 104
7.3 Assessing the Mechanisms 105
    7.3.1 Availability 105
    7.3.2 Message Complexity 106
    7.3.3 Migration Delay 107
    7.3.4 Overall Assessment 109
7.4 Discussion 110

8 Conclusion 111
8.1 Future Work 113

A	**Fundamentals of Probability Theory**	**115**
B	**Introduction to Fault Tolerance**	**119**
	B.1 Basic Concepts and Definitions	119
	B.2 Failure Classification	122
C	**Fault Tolerance and Message Complexity**	**125**
	C.1 The Energy Concept	125
	C.2 The Path Concept	126
	C.3 The Shadow Protocol	129
D	**Bibliography**	**143**

List of Figures

The agent model 15
Locating agents: different mechanisms. 19
Energy concept: energy consumption of services 26
Path concept: creating the path upon migration 30
Shadows: the creation of a shadow 34
Shadows: requesting a new time quantum 34
Shadows: unsuccessful request for new time quantum 34
Shadows: creating a new agent 35
Shadows: regular update of proxy paths 36
Hierarchical shadows 42
Hierarchical shadows: fine-grained control 42
Hierarchical shadows: locating an agent 45
Shadows: high communication costs 49
Mobile shadows: the moving shadow 50
Mobile shadows: update of proxy paths 51
Mobile shadows: agent losing shadow proxy 51
Shadow concept: path availability 63
Shadow concept: basic protocol vs. path concept 64
Simple reference counting 68
The Lermen & Maurer variant 69
The Rudalics variant with 3 messages 71
The Rudalics variant with 4 messages 72
Weighted reference counting 74
Local reference counting 76
Simple reference counting 82
Optimized transformation of simple reference counting 83
Lermen & Maurer variant 84
Optimized transformation of the Lermen & Maurer variant 85
Rudalics 3 message variant 86
Optimized transformation of Rudalics 3-message variant 87
Weighted reference counting 88
Local reference counting 89
Optimized transformation of local reference counting 90
Direct reference counting 92
Direct reference counting optimized 93
Local reference counting 94
Local reference counting optimized 95
Local reference counting and weighted reference counting 100
Classification of the different mechanisms 104
Control mechanisms: functionality vs. availability 105

The message complexity of the different classified types 106
Control mechanisms: functionality vs. message complexity 107
Control mechanisms: functionality vs. migration delay 108
Control mechanisms: combining the assessments 109
Exponential distribution of density and probability 117
Availability function for a single component 121
Failure classification. 123
Path concept: the availability of a path depending on λ and n 127

List of Algorithms and Tables

Energy concept: basic place methods 27
Energy concept: agent methods 28
Energy concept: system methods...28
Path concept: creating a trail 31
Path concept: methods for finding agents 31
Path concept: shortening the path 32
Shadows: system methods 37
Shadows: the check phase..38
Shadows: methods in the shadow object 39
Shadows: reaction to time-outs 40
Shadows: locating agents 40
Hierarchical shadows: extended methods for regular intervals 43
Hierarchical shadows: the shadow's check phase 43
Hierarchical shadows: additional shadow methods 44
Hierarchical shadows: reaction to time-outs..44
Hierarchical shadows: propagating a find request 46
Hierarchical shadows: collecting the answers for a find request.........................48
Hierarchical shadows: reaction to time-outs when locating agents 48
Mobile shadows: mobility and communication...53
Mobile shadows: extended methods for regular intervals 54
Mobile shadows: checking the shadow 55
Mobile shadows: extending the agent's life...55
Mobile shadows: detecting terminated agents 56
Failure and repair rates for components (in hours)..62
Reference manipulation by objects 67
Simple reference counting 69
The Lermen & Maurer variant 70
The Rudalics variant with 3 messages 71
The Rudalics variant with 4 messages 73
Weighted reference counting 75
Local reference counting..77
The basic computations of an agent...80
Simple reference counting transformed 82
The Lermen & Maurer variant transformed...85
Rudalics 3 message variant transformed..87
Weighted reference counting transformed...89
Local reference counting transformed 91
Direct reference counting transformed 93
Local reference counting transformed 96
Properties of the transformations: agents as parent objects 97

Properties of the transformations: dependency objects as parent objects.........98
Properties of the combinations..99
Combination of WRC and LRC..101
Properties of the useful transformations 102
Functionality of the different mechanisms 103

Abbreviations

ACM	Association for Computing Machinery
AI	Artificial Intelligence
API	Application Programming Interface
CORBA	Common Object Request Broker Architecture
DAI	Distributed Artificial Intelligence
DGC	Distributed Garbage Collection
DNS	Domain Name System
DRC	Direct Reference Counting
FIFO	First-In First-Out
FIPA	Foundation for Intelligent Physical Agents
HTML	Hypertext Markup Language
HTTP	HyperText Transfer Protocol
IEEE	Institute of Electrical and Electronics Engineers
ISO	International Organization for Standardization
LAN	Local Area Network
LRC	Local Reference Counting
MAF	Mobile Agent Facility
MASIF	Mobile Agent System Interoperability Facility
MA	Mobile Agents
MAS	Mobile Agent Systems
OMA	Object Management Architecture
OMG	Open Management Group
ORB	Object Request Broker
RC	Reference Counting
RPC	Remote Procedure Call
SSP Chains	Stub Scion Pair Chains
TCP	Transmission Control Protocol
URL	Uniform Resource Locator
WAN	Wide Area Network
WRC	Weighted Reference Counting
WWW	World Wide Web

> *"Where shall I begin, please your Majesty?"*
> *he asked.*
> *"Begin at the beginning,"* the King said,
> *gravely, "and go on till you come to the end;*
> *then stop."*
>
> Lewis Carrol, Alice in Wonderland

1 Introduction

The Internet is widely advertised as *the* solution for all problems having to do with information retrieval and electronic commerce. The common belief is that nearly everything can be found and/or bought on the Internet. Moreover, the Internet itself is imagined to have technical qualities that are nearly magical (at least by those who never used it): unlimited bandwidth, no network latency, reliable communication are only a few of these. However, many of the technological problems of the Internet have still to be solved before belief and reality meet. Besides limited bandwidth and unreliable communication without quality-of-service guarantees, one of the most difficult questions is how to deal with the dynamics of an ever-changing and daily growing environment. Furthermore, mobility plays an increasing role. The problems associated with it are manifold: a mobile device is frequently disconnected, be it through communication failures, e.g. because the device communicating over a wireless network enters a screened area, or because the user unplugged its network connection. It is neither foreseeable when and whether the device connects back, nor if it is connected back to the same network, e.g. if the device is transported from Europe to Asia. These extra difficulties add considerably to the gravity of the Internet's problems.

On top of the Internet with all of its problems the World Wide Web has been established. The World Wide Web provides access to information structured to some extent with hyperlinks. But with every passing day it is less suited to organize a tremendous and ever growing amount of data, that at times only incidentally conveys useful information. To make matters even more complex, an electronic commerce infrastructure begins to emerge from the World Wide Web, that has to support a secure means of online transactions with fault semantics that differ considerably from those of the underlying network, the Internet. Additionally this electronic commerce infrastructure is orders of magnitude larger than every traditional distributed system, for which solutions providing secure online transactions exist.

Thus in a situation that becomes worse with every day traditional distributed systems have no ready answer to solve the problems of the Internet, the World Wide Web and the emerging electronic commerce systems.

In this situation, a shift in the underlying computing paradigm seems necessary to provide a fresh and unobstructed point of view to find new solutions for these problems. One of the new, encouraging paradigms studied in detail is the mobile agent paradigm. Mobile agents promise to deal more efficiently and elegantly with the dynamic, heterogeneous, and open environment, which is today's Internet.

A mobile agent is an active entity that can act within a distributed system of agent places on behalf of its user, following a given task. A place provides an abstract representation of a host and its services. The agent can autonomously migrate from one place in the network to another during its execution. While it computes, it is able to observe its environment and to adapt dynamically to changes. It can continue its computations asynchronously even if the user that has started it is (temporarily) not connected to the distributed system any more, i.e. the mobile agent paradigm is able to support mobile computing quite naturally. By moving the agent to the host on which data resides, communication latency may be reduced in many cases. Furthermore, by processing the data and sending only the relevant results, the consumption of bandwidth and/or the connection time can be reduced, which is again an advantage for mobile computing.

Applications for mobile agents are widespread and encompass not only applications in electronic commerce environments and applications to search and filter global information spaces, but can also be found in the areas of network management, monitoring, information dissemination or parallel processing. These are only some of the application areas on which many different authors agree, e.g. ROTHERMEL AND SCHWEHM (1998), FÜNFROCKEN AND MATTERN (1999), WONG, PACIOREK AND MOORE (1999) and LANGE AND OSHIMA (1999) consider these and other application areas.

In all of these applications mechanisms are needed that provide the user with the ability to control mobile agents. Control mechanisms can have the following functionality:

- *Finding agents*. For example, if an agent has been sent out, and the user requests a status report, then the agent has to be located somehow to allow a detailed examination.
- *Termination of agents*. If a user decides that an agent is no longer used, then the system should allow the user-controlled termination of the agent.
- *Orphan detection*. If an agent has become an orphan, then the system should detect this and remove it. To detect an orphan, a relationship is needed that can be exploited to derive the status of an agent. In contrast to e.g. client/server systems no natural relationship between mobile agents, or between mobile agents and objects outside the mobile agent system exists. Hence an artificial definition of such a relationship has to be introduced to allow orphan detection.

In this book, we will define a relationship between an agent and a dependency object that allows the detection of orphans. The dependency object might be another agent, a system structure or something else. Based on this we will propose different mechanisms providing functionality for locating agents, for terminating them, and for orphan detection.

In the area of mobile agent systems the current research concentrates on the implementation of basic systems, i.e. systems supporting simple communication and migration. Only slowly the problem area of control algorithms for mobile agents is beginning to evoke the interest of the research community. The approaches published are not very complex and do not fully take into account the unique situation of a widely distributed system with unreliable communication and frequently disconnected devices. One example is an approach that implements a brute force search of the whole distributed system, which is comparable to a broadcast to all nodes of the Internet. Another approach is to try and guess the agent's location. The system and failure models of these approaches are still a bit idealized and do not fully fit the situation in the Internet. In this book we will concentrate on mechanisms based on a system and a failure model conforming to the existing Internet.

First the energy concept is presented, which supports orphan detection for mobile agents. In this concept every agent gets some energy. Every action the agent takes, every service that is used, costs energy. When the energy is used up, the agent is an orphan and can be removed by the system. Locating an agent or terminating it is not possible with this concept.

Then the path concept will be discussed, a variant of which is used in the area of distributed systems to track mobile objects. This concept provides functionality for locating agents and for their termination, but offers no orphan detection functionality. Every agent leaves a path in the system, i.e. whenever an agent migrates, information is left behind about the agent's target place. The path can be followed to find the agent, and/or to terminate it.

The third concept presented is the shadow concept. This concept supports locating and terminating of mobile agents and furthermore, provides orphan detection functionality. It combines the energy concept and the path concept in a way that leaves the agents most of their autonomy, has low communication costs, and provides excellent fault tolerance (i.e. a high availability). An agent leaves a trail in the system, but in contrast to the trail in the path concept, this trail is cut short in regular intervals. To allow for simple locating and termination of agents, a delegate of the application is left in the system, the shadow. As long as the shadow exists, all dependent agents are allowed to continue their work, i.e. the agents are no longer depending on the availability of the application. Thus no permanent connection between agents and application is needed, an application can e.g. run only intermittently to check for results.

In the area of distributed algorithms mechanisms have been developed to solve similar problems (i.e. termination detection and distributed garbage collection). TEL AND MATTERN (1993) proved that the class of termination detection algorithms and the class of garbage collection algorithms are identical. Using a transformation, an algorithm of one class can be changed into an algorithm of the other class and vice versa. In fact, new algorithms were discovered this way.

A similar transformation providing the conversion of either of these classes into control algorithms for mobile agents should allow access to a large number of algorithms for controlling mobile agents. But the failure model of the area of distributed algorithms and of the area of mobile agents are radically different, ruling out the direct use of these mechanisms.

Instead we will use transformed garbage collection algorithms to show the following: all the principles of the transformed algorithms can be found in the control mechanisms proposed in this book or in the literature. Furthermore, the proposed control algorithms show elements (e.g. the timed paths of the shadow concept) that are not found in garbage collection algorithms. This ensures that, even if the failure model is still different, the class of garbage collection algorithms is a subset of the class of control algorithms for mobile agents. Furthermore, if a new, radically different algorithm is developed either in the area of termination detection or in the area of distributed garbage collection, it can be transformed at once and its principles can be exploited for developing new control mechanisms for mobile agents.

Finally the control mechanisms are compared with mechanisms presented in the literature regarding reliability, message complexity, interference with the agent autonomy and usability for applications.

Over hill, over dale,
*   Thorough bush, thorough brier,*
Over park, over pale,
*   Thorough flood, thorough fire,*
I do wander every where,
Swifter than the moone's sphere.

W. Shakespeare, Midsummer-Night's Dream

2 Mobile Agents

Due to its notable properties the mobile agent paradigm has received a rapid growth in attention over the last few years. The research community involved in the area of mobile agents is steadily growing, and more and more systems are being developed in both academia and industry. Moreover, standardization efforts for mobile agent facilities and architectures are already in progress.

These architectures have to provide functionality for agent migration, communication of agents with other agents and with the underlying system, and for agent control (i.e. to start agents, to stop agents, to find agents etc.). While support for agent migration and for communication between agents is provided by nearly all mobile agent systems, support for control mechanisms (apart from the ability to start agents) is neglected in most existing systems so far.

Depending on the application in which the mobile agent paradigm is to be used, additional support for security or for transactions is necessary. Since we concentrate on control mechanisms in this book, we will not discuss these further. The interested reader is referred to HOHL (1997) regarding security, and to ROTHERMEL AND STRASSER (1998) regarding a mechanism providing exactly-once semantics for mobile agents.

This chapter first gives a short introduction to mobile agents, including a short history, a discussion of properties of mobile agents and of applications using mobile agents. Examples of mobile agent systems will provide us with an understanding of the similarities between the different approaches. This understanding allows to define a minimal agent model that provides a common ground for all the existing systems. By using this agent model as the basis for developing our mechanisms, it is ensured that they can be used in all these systems (and most probably in other existing systems as well). We will then assert why control mechanisms for mobile agents are of importance if applications are to be used successfully in an open environment like the Internet. We will examine why control mechanisms for mobile agents have to be different from those for classical distributed systems. Finally, we will give an overview over the work in the area of mobile agents which relates to control aspects.

2.1 Introduction to Mobile Agents

2.1.1 A Short History of Mobile Agents

The idea to send machine independent executable messages via a network can be traced back to the very beginning of the Internet, where the Decode-Encode-Language DEL was considered for running interactive programs on remote consoles of a networked system (RULIFSON (1969)). Later the idea emerged independently in the area of radio network communication, where the SOFTNET project used Forth-messages to transmit data as well as to reprogram the underlying network. Details can be found in ZANDER (1981). Another early approach was the Network Command Language by FALCONE (1987).

In the early eighties a new communication paradigm, the concept of the *remote procedure call*, introduced by BIRRELL AND NELSON (1984), became increasingly popular, and led to today's prevalent architectural model for distributed systems, the client/server model. STAMOS AND GIFFORD (1990) combined the RPC and the idea of executable messages into a concept called *remote evaluation*. Here a process passes not only the parameters of the called procedure but the code of the procedure as well.

In the beginning of the nineties the term 'messengers' was used by TSCHUDIN (1993) to denote active messages programmed in his Postscript-like language M0. The term 'mobile agent' was finally coined in a white paper by General Magic Inc. in 1994 (republished in WHITE (1997)). The idea described there was so appealing that it initiated research all over the world.

General Magic's Telescript language was specifically designed for mobile agent programming and already included most of the concepts of later mobile agent systems, but it was dropped when it became clear that it could not compete with Java (see SUN (1994) and SUN (1999) for details) as a commercial product. In the sequel several mobile agent systems have been developed in the research community. In the beginning the research systems were based on diverse programming languages, e.g. Agent Tcl, which is based on the scripting language Tcl (see GRAY ET AL. (1996) and GRAY (1997) for a description). Today most of the existing systems are based on Java. Examples are Mole, developed at the University of Stuttgart or Aglets by the IBM Aglets Workbench Team. Details regarding Mole can be found in BAUMANN ET AL. (1998A) and an introduction to Aglets is given in LANGE AND OSHIMA (1998). Other approaches use a language independent approach like TACOMA by JOHANSEN ET AL. (1995) or Ara by PEINE AND STOLPMANN (1997). Recently, several companies and research groups have promoted MASIF, an OMG standard for mobile agent systems (see MILOJICIC ET AL. (1998)). A short description of these systems will be given in Chapter 2.2. Interestingly, one of the companies supporting the MASIF standard is General Magic Inc., where in the meantime a Java-based mobile agent system called Odyssey has been developed. Details to Odyssey can be found in GENERAL MAGIC (1997).

2.1.2 Properties of Mobile Agents

The mobile agent paradigm provides some very interesting properties, which are very important for applications employing mobile agents (see next section). The mobile agent paradigm

- *supports asynchronous and autonomous operation.*
  A mobile agent does not need a permanent connection to its owner, i.e. the device of the owner; it performs its task asynchronously. Asynchronous communication mechanisms, such as asynchronous message queues (e.g. see IBM (1999A)), are used in classical distributed systems as well, but there the client performing a task must be available to receive incoming messages and react to them, i.e. it needs a permanent connection. This can be very problematic e.g. if the client is located on a mobile device. By employing the mobile agent paradigm, a task can be encapsulated in an agent created on the mobile device while disconnected. This agent is then launched into the network, where it performs its task. Necessarily, the mobile device has to connect to the network for this. The agent now autonomously follows the given task. Clearly, the mobile device can be disconnected as soon as the agent is transferred. Later, the mobile device can reconnect to accept the results of the agent's task.
- *allows dynamic and flexible adaptation to a changing environment.*
  Mobile agents can examine their execution environment, and adapt dynamically to changes, e.g. by using different services. If a service needed (e.g. a database) is not accessible, then the agent may choose to use a combination of other services to access the same information, or it may move to another host in the network. This service might even be the execution environment itself.
- *allows reduction of communication costs.*
  By transferring an agent across the network to the source of data to process it there, the communication bandwidth and communication latency can be reduced. An example is the processing of weather data, where sometimes large amounts of data have to be processed with varying algorithms. One way to solve this problem is to transfer the data over the network. If instead an agent is moved to the systems hosting the weather data, only the results of the processing have to be sent back. This is done with the system TACOMA (see JOHANSEN ET AL. (1995) for an introduction).
- *allows encapsulation of protocols.*
  The Internet's fast growth has increased the number of computers, protocols and data formats for data exchange to a point, where it is cumbersome if not impossible to upgrade protocol code properly. As a result, protocols often become a legacy problem. Mobile agents permit new protocols to be installed automatically, and only as needed for a particular interaction.
- *provides support for fault-tolerant computing.*
  The potential of a mobile agent to react dynamically to unfavourable situations makes it easier to build robust and fault-tolerant distributed systems. An agent can e.g. be instructed how to solve problems such as services that are no longer

provided by using alternate services, or failing communication channels e.g. by using other servers providing the needed service.

As has been pointed out by CHESS ET AL. (1997), most of these properties could be achieved by other means, but not in this combination, and not while offering the flexibility provided by the mobile agent paradigm.

2.1.3 Applications

No single killer application employing mobile agent technology has been identified yet, but applications exist that profit considerably from the mobile agent paradigm. Many of these have been pointed out by authors such as CHESS ET AL. (1997), ROTHERMEL AND SCHWEHM (1998), FÜNFROCKEN AND MATTERN (1999), WONG, PACIOREK AND MOORE (1999) and LANGE AND OSHIMA (1999).

The most interesting of these applications are:

- *Electronic commerce.*
  Electronic commerce is certainly one of the most attractive application areas: a commercial transaction may require real-time access to remote resources, such as stock quotes, and fast reactions which are not impeded by a slow network. A mobile agent can act and negotiate on behalf of its user, buying, selling, or trading goods, services or information. One example for an e-commerce platform with mobile agents is TabiCan (see IBM (1997)), an electronic marketplace framework based on IBM aglets.
- *Distributed information retrieval.*
  Instead of moving large amounts of data through the network to extract the needed information on the client side, an agent can be sent to remote information sources, where the information can be extracted locally. This is especially valuable, if the information to be extracted cannot be anticipated exactly. A mobile agent can incorporate an implementation of a specific search algorithm that extracts the data, and move to the location of the data, thus allowing for semantic information compression locally. In particular, when information spread across multiple sites has to be related, the mobile agent paradigm is beneficial. In THEILMANN AND ROTHERMEL (1999) this application of mobile agents has been discussed. In combination with parallel processing, i.e. by employing more than one agent, and a coordination concept (e.g. see BAUMANN AND RADOUNIKLIS (1997)) distributed information retrieval is considerably facilitated.
- *Monitoring.*
  An agent can be sent out to monitor a given information source or wait for a specific event. As soon as a change occurs, the agent reacts according to its programming; it e.g. sends a message or buys shares on a stock market. Another example is the monitoring and management of network devices (e.g. see BALDI, GAI AND PICCO (1997) for a discussion). The advantages of mobile agents in this applica-

tion area are the flexibility of the agent's programming and the asynchronous and autonomous execution.
- *Workflow management systems.*
  In workflow applications the flow of data between coworkers characterizes the processing of information. Mobile agents are especially useful here because they provide mobility, behaviour, information about the workflow and autonomy to every workflow item. Thus the workflow becomes independent of a particular workflow application. Moreover, the agent can provide all code necessary to access the items' information in a semantically correct manner. SCHÜTZNER (1999) is an example of integrating mobile agents with workflows.
- *Information dissemination.*
  Mobile agents can disseminate information (e.g. news) to a number of customers. They provide access policies, which e.g. ensure that an article can only be read after the customer has paid for it. Additionally they implement the functionality needed to show the news article in the way best suited to article and output medium, e.g. computer or PDA screen, or printer. One example of an information dissemination infrastructure has been described in KONSTANTAS ET AL. (1996).
- *Parallel processing.*
  In principle, parallel processes can be distributed by mobile agents very easily. The mobile agents distributing the computation might even redistribute themselves to adapt to changes in the environment. A framework to allow transparent distribution of computations over a network of mobile agent systems has been presented in STRASSER, BAUMANN AND SCHWEHM (1999). Using such a framework, all computations which can be split into smaller, autonomously computable parts can be distributed automatically, thus employing the full computational capacity of a network of computers.
- *Software deployment.*
  Mobile agents can be used to automate the process of software installation and software updates. Before transporting the software package itself to the target computer, an agent can gather information about the environment in which the software will be installed, e.g. its version and additional packages. It can query the user for installation preferences, uncompress and compile the software, and watch for future software updates.

2.2 Examples of Mobile Agent Systems

We will now briefly examine the different systems mentioned above. We will concentrate on the functionality directly influencing the respective agent model. This information can then be used to derive a minimal agent model based on the different approaches. By using this minimal agent model it can be ensured that the mechanisms developed in this book are usable in all of these systems.

2.2.1 High-Level Language-Based Systems

2.2.1.1 Telescript

Telescript is a language that has been developed particularly for the programming of mobile agents by General Magic Inc. in 1994. WHITE (1997) gives an introduction to Telescript. It consists of two parts, an object-oriented language called High Telescript, and a virtual machine code called Low Telescript, into which High Telescript is compiled. Unlike Java, Telescript focuses on the concept of a process with its associated concepts of ownership of objects and execution state. Thus, Telescript avoids many of today's problems with Java-based agent systems, some of which are the lack of support for resource control, and the lack of support for retrieving the full execution state of an object. Central concepts are the place process and the agent process. Places can contain other processes, i.e. both places and agents. All processes have globally unique, immutable names. Agents can move between places to communicate with other agents or to use services provided by the place.

Agents on the same place can communicate via a session concept called *meet*. A meeting requires a *petition*, data that specifies the agent to be met and other terms of the meeting. This includes e.g. the time by which it must begin. The meeting can fail either because one of the terms of the meeting cannot be satisfied, or because the target agent declines the meeting.

Agents on different places communicate via *connections*. Here the agent to be connected has to specified together with the place on which it is to be found. Additional terms of the connection can be specified. An example of such an additional term is the quality of the service that has to be provided. As with meetings, the connection can fail either because one of the terms cannot be met, or because the target agent is not interested in a connection and declines.

Additionally, Telescript introduces the concept of the *authority* of a process, i.e. of either an agent or a place. The authority of an agent or place is essentially the owner of the respective process. The owner can either be an individual or an organization. A process can determine its own authority, but so can every other process. Withholding or falsifying the own authority is impossible.

Using this concept of authority, Telescript defines *regions*, which are collections of places operated by the same authority. Whenever an agent migrates from one region to another, the source region has to prove the authority of the agent to the target region of the migration. If the source region fails to prove the authority, or if the target region is not interested to accept agents of this particular authority, then the migration fails, i.e. the agent is denied the entry into the target region.

The concept of authority now allows to restrict the access to places or regions to agents of specific authorities. The same holds true for agents: by determining the authority of a place an agent is about to visit, it can restrict itself to places with authorities considered safe. Finally the contact between agents can be restricted to certain authorities. For instance, if a meeting is received from an agent with questionable authority, then this request can be declined without further communication.

Every authority can limit the rights of processes by assigning *permits* to them. A permit grants capabilities, which can be determined by a process, but cannot be increased. Two kinds of capabilities are distinguished: first, the capability to execute a certain instruction (e.g. the creation of an agent), and second, the capability to use a resource to a certain extent. Capabilities of the second kind are maximum lifetime, maximum size or a maximum amount of computation time. As soon as one of these capabilities is exceeded, the process is terminated. Please note that this holds true for places as well as for agents. Whenever an agent arrives at a new place, its effective permit is computed by combining the permits of agent, place and region. This allows to place general access restrictions for a region into its associated permit, and to add individual restrictions to the places on a case-by-case basis.

2.2.1.2 Mole

Mole is probably the first Java-based mobile agent systems and was developed at the University of Stuttgart (see BAUMANN ET AL. (1998B)). Agents in Mole have immutable, globally unique names and can provide or request services, which can be announced and looked up locally. They can migrate between different places, which are an abstraction of a host, to meet other agents and to access services provided by agents or places.

Agents can be addressed either through their globally unique name or through *badges*, which can be put on or removed at will. The badge concept allows to identify an agent by using a symbolic, not necessarily unique name. A badge is an application-generated identifier, such as "Printing Service", which agents can "pin on" and "pin off". This badge represents a role of an agent at a given time. As long as the agent provides the functionality associated with this role it wears the badge.

Mole supports many different communication mechanisms, e.g. simple messages, RPC-like communication, or session mechanisms, both locally and globally. A session defines a communication relationship between a pair of agents. After session setup, the agents can interact by remote method invocation or by message passing. When all information has been communicated, the session is terminated. Sessions have the following characteristics:

- Sessions may be intra-place as well as inter-place communication relationships, i.e., two agents participating in a session are not required to reside at the same place.
- In order to preserve the autonomy of agents, each session peer must explicitly agree to participate in the session. Further, an agent may unilaterally terminate the sessions it is involved in at any point in time.
- While an agent is involved in a session, it is not supposed to move to another place. However, if it decides to move anyway, the session is terminated implicit-

ly. The main reason for this property is to simplify the underlying communication mechanism, e.g., to avoid the need for message forwarding.

Detailed information about the different communication concepts of Mole can be found in BAUMANN ET AL. (1997).

2.2.1.3 The Aglets Workbench

Another Java-based system is the Aglets workbench, created at the IBM Tokyo Research Laboratory (see IBM (1999B)). An aglet is a combination of the applet model and the agent model, adding mobility to applets. While this approach allows an applet programmer to quickly grasp the functionality of aglets, it constrains aglets to a mainly event-based model. Aglets have immutable, globally unique names and can communicate with other aglets via messages. Aglets can migrate between *contexts* (the framework's term for a place) to access services provided by the context or to communicate with other agents.

Communication can be local and global, synchronous or asynchronous. To communicate with an aglet, a representative, the *AgletProxy*, is used, that offers methods to send synchronous or asynchronous messages. It serves as a shield that protects the aglet against direct access to its public methods. It also provides location transparencey; regardless of the location of the aglet, the message is forwarded to the aglet by the AgletProxy.

If a message is sent synchronously, then the method provided by the AgletProxy blocks until a result is received. In the case of asynchronous messages two variants are distinguished: messages without a reply and messages with a reply. In the second case the aglet sending the message has to determine at a later time, whether a reply has already been received. To allow this, the AgletProxy returns an object called FutureReply, which can be examined to check whether the reply has already arrived. If this is the case, the FutureReply object can be used to receive this reply.

2.2.2 Language-Independent Systems

2.2.2.1 D'Agents

D'Agents is a mobile agent system that was originally based on the typeless scripting language Tcl (Tool command language). It has been developed by GRAY ET AL. (1996) at the Dartmouth College.

The architecture of D'agents has a four-level core system. The different layers are: the transport mechanism layer (for migration and communication), an agent server layer (which implements the place concept), an interpreter layer, in which an interpreter for every supported language runs, and the agent layer. The agent server provides only lew-level functionality for migration and for communication. All other functionality, including higher-level communication mechanisms, name server functionality, or service directories, have to be implemented as agents. Agents providing some of this functionality (e.g. an agent RPC) are provided with the system.

A disadvantage of the design of D'Agents is that an agent name contains its network location, i.e. while globally unique, it is not immutable. This makes it problematic to reliably identify an agent that migrates. Thus some kind of tracking mechanism is essential, but has to be provided by the programmer.

2.2.2.2 TACOMA

The TACOMA (Tromsø And COrnell Moving Agents) system is a language-independent mobile agent system that supports agents written in Tcl, C, C++, Perl, Scheme and others (see JOHANSEN ET AL. (1995) for a description). Two main low-level mechanisms are characteristic for TACOMA: *folders*, where agents store data, and the *meet* operation which, in contrast to the meet semantics in other agent systems, starts another agent and transfers a folder as an argument. The execution of the calling agent is blocked until the *meet* operation terminates. This means, that agents that are already running cannot communicate with each other. Furthermore, an agent starting a *meet* operation, depends on the called agent ending the *meet* operation for its own continued operation.

Folders contain elements, each of which is an uninterpreted sequence of bits. When an agent wants to migrate from one host to another (the place concept does not exist in TACOMA), it can put folders into its *briefcase*, which is transported to the new host, where a new instance of the agent is started with the briefcase as an argument. Data can also left behind by agents in site-local folders, which are collected in *file cabinets*.

2.2.2.3 ARA

The ARA (Agents for Remote Action) system is a mobile agent platform that has been developed at the University of Kaiserslautern by PEINE AND STOLPMANN (1997). ARA follows a language-independent approach: Tcl, C and Java are the languages supported at the moment. The programming model of ARA consists of agents moving between places, where they use services provided by the host or other agents.

A place is physically located on one host machine, and may impose specific security restrictions on the agents entering that place in the form of a local allowance limiting the agent's resource accesses while staying at that place. Besides that, an agent may also be equipped with a global allowance by its principal (a principal being an agent user, an agent programmer, or a host machine), controlling the agent's behavior throughout its lifetime. This allows to program agents similar to normal programs in most respects, i.e. when accessing a file system, interacting via a user interface or communicating over the network.

Agents have globally unique identifiers, which can be used to send remote messages or can be employed for local client/server communication. Higher communication mechanisms must be built on top of these mechanisms.

An interesting functionality of the ARA system is the support for creation of *agent checkpoints*. Agents can create, at any time of their execution, a checkpoint, which contains the information of their current internal state. This checkpoint is stored on stable storage, and allows to later restore the agent to its state at the moment of checkpointing. This functionality allows to build fault tolerance schemes that, before letting the agent undertake a "risky" operation (e.g. migrating to a host that crashes from time to time), create a backup copy that can be used if the agent is lost.

2.2.3 Standardization Efforts

At the moment there are various standardization efforts in progress, some of which are driven by the AGENT SOCIETY (1999) or by the FIPA (1999). But the most interesting of the standardization efforts is MASIF, the OMG Mobile Agent System Interoperability Facility (see MILOJICIC ET AL. (1998) for a description of the standard), which is backed by many of the companies and research institutes involved in the mobile agent field.

MASIF tries to define a minimal interoperable interface for mobile agent systems. Communication is not addressed in the standard, i.e. left to CORBA standards. Agents in the MASIF standard can migrate between places, and they have a unique identifier. The standard is naturally focusing on CORBA as a system infrastructure (e.g. for serialization), but does not enforce it as a means of communication. Furthermore mechanisms for locating agents are presented in the standard (see Chapter 2.5 for a discussion).

2.3 Our Agent Model

The agent model used in this book contains only those properties that are either common to the mobile agent systems presented above, or can be provided by them without problems. The agent models of the systems discussed above are based on the concepts of places and agents (see Figure 2-1). Some systems use a different terminology to describe these concepts (see above), but we will use the terms adopted by the majority of mobile agent systems.

Places provide the environment for executing mobile agents. Additionally, they may provide abstractions of services of the underlying node. A place is entirely located on a single node of the underlying network. An agent system consists of a number of these places.

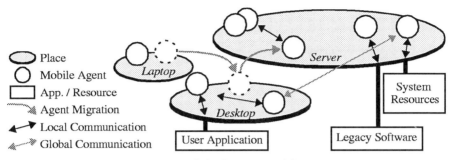

Figure 2-1. The agent model

Mobile agents are active entities, which may move from place to place to meet other agents and to access the places' services. An agent can be created either by an application outside the agent system, or by another agent. An agent can be identified by a globally unique agent identifier, which is generated at the agent's creation time and is not changed throughout its life. The place on which the agent has been created can be derived from the identifier. Communication between agents may be local or global.

2.3.1 Relations between Agents

In the course of this book we will need the concept of a dependency between mobile agents, but in mobile agent systems no natural relationship exists that would allow to derive dependencies between the mobile agents. In other areas of the field of distributed systems these relationships are common. There *natural* relationships between the participants of the system are used to derive the dependencies. Typical relationships are:

- the client/server relationship, in which a server activity has a clear relation to a request sent by a client (e.g. see TANENBAUM (1995) or COMER AND STEVENS (1993)).
- the parent/child relationship of migrating processes in distributed systems, where a process has at any time a parent process it depends on, i.e. the process that created it. One example for a system using such a relationship is the distributed system Sprite, which is described in DOUGLIS AND OUSTERHOUT (1991).
- the reference relationship in the area of distributed garbage collection, where some distinguished objects, called root objects, are needed by the computation, e.g. because they interact with the user. If an object is reachable directly or indirectly, by following references from the root object, it is called alive. Only objects which are alive can affect the result of the computation (see SHAPIRO ET AL. (1994) for an introduction).

The dependency provided by these relationships allows to decide whether a dependent process, thread or object can be declared to be an orphan and can be removed. Since nothing comparable exists for mobile agents, a concept has to be provided that supports such a relationship. To that end we now introduce the concept of a *dependency object*:

Definition 2-1: Dependency Object

> A dependency object is an object that provides a parent relation to another object.

The dependency object can be an agent, an object on a place, or even the place itself. Let us denote a child as being an object which depends on a dependency object. This dependency object is then the child's parent. The child is not necessarily limited to exactly one dependency object.

We assume that a child agent needs the existence of at least one of its dependency objects. Based on this assumption we can define an orphan agent as:

Definition 2-2: Orphan

> An agent is an orphan when no dependency object relates to it.

2.3.1.1 A Group Concept with the Dependency Object

To illustrate the generality of the concept of dependency objects, we define a group concept, in which an agent depends on the existence of the group of which it is a member. The following definition is only one of many possible definitions of a group and an orphan agent employing the dependency object.

Let us see an agent group as a collection of mobile agents pursuing a common goal. We define that no agent exists without an associated group. An agent without a group is an orphan and can be removed from the system. Each group has an associated group object γ, that represents the group, and exists exactly as long as the group exists. This group object is realized as a dependency object. If an agent joins a group then the group object is established as a new dependency object of the joining agent. A group of agents will be denoted as G_γ, an agent belonging to a group G_γ as A_γ. Let us indicate that an agent A depends on a group object γ with $A \rightarrow \gamma$. Then a group can be defined as

$$G_\gamma = \{A | A \rightarrow \gamma\}$$

with G_γ as an agent group containing all agents A that depend on the group object γ (i.e. all A_γ). An agent can be a member of more than one group. In that case it is no orphan as long as at least any one of the groups, i.e. one of the associated group objects, exists. The set of groups an agent is member of can be defined as

$$M_A = \{G_\gamma | A \rightarrow \gamma\}$$

with M_A as the set of all groups G_γ for which the agent A depends on the group objects γ. Now an orphan is an agent for which the following condition holds true:

$$A \text{ is orphan} \Leftrightarrow M_A = \{\varnothing\}$$

2.4 Control Mechanisms for Mobile Agents

We define control mechanisms for mobile agents as mechanisms that provide at least one of the following functionalities:

- *locating agents.* A mechanism for locating agents returns either the current location of the agent, or the information that the agent does not exist anymore. In many applications the ability to get information about the computation in progress, i.e. to get status information from the working agents, or to interact with the agents, e.g. to change their behaviour, is essential. To do this reliably and with acceptable costs, mechanisms have to be used that locate the agent in order to communicate.

  To interact with an agent, in principle an alternative to explicitly locate the agent exists. By employing an anonymous group communication mechanism the agent would not have to be located. Examples for anonymous group communication mechanisms are distributed tuple spaces (for an introduction to tuple spaces see CARRIERO AND GELERNTER (1989)) or distributed event channels as defined by the OMG. BAUMANN ET AL. (1997) present different possible applications for this type of communication. But these mechanisms either provide only best-effort semantics, or are extremely expensive if reliable communication is needed. BECK (1997) and KUBACH (1998) discuss the problem of communication with mobile participants in more detail. Since the existing mechanisms are neither designed for mobile participants nor designed to communicate with *one* mobile participant efficiently, a mechanism that is explicitly designed to locate a mobile agent will provide the same functionality with less communication costs.

- *detection of orphan agents.* A mechanism that provides orphan detection functionality decides whether an agent is an orphan according to Definition 2-2. By employing such a mechanism a mobile agent system can remove orphan agents, thus reclaiming occupied resources.

  In a commercial environment, or in an environment with limited resources, it is important that only as many resources as needed are used. Consider the following scenario: an agent A on a place P creates child agents that search for prices of VCRs in a distributed database and report the results back to agent A. Place P crashes and the agent A is lost. The child agents are no longer able to report their findings, and unnecessarily consume resources. By detecting that the child agents are orphans the system can remove them and thus minimize the resource consumption.

- *termination of agents.* A mechanism providing this functionality allows an agent to be stopped and removed from the system, regardless of the agent's location. For example, if the results of a mobile agent searching a distributed data base are no longer relevant, or if an agent monitoring an information source is no longer needed, then the agent could be terminated. One possibility to implement a mechanism for terminating agents is to use a mechanism to locate the agent and to send the termination command to it subsequently. But it would be even better to have a mechanism for locating agents that has been designed with this application in mind, a mechanism that could deliver this command immediately when it locates the agent.

To summarize our findings, the different functionalities that can be part of control mechanisms are needed by applications or by the user, and should be provided by every mobile agent system.

2.5 Related Work in the Area of Mobile Agents

As has been said before, support for control mechanisms has been neglected in most mobile agent systems so far (apart from functionality for creating agents). The two exceptions are the MASIF standard and the Aglets Workbench. We will now give an overview of the provided mechanisms, first for locating agents, then for orphan detection, and finally for termination.

2.5.1 Locating Agents

Different potential mechanisms for locating agents can be identified, depending on the assumptions about migrational behaviour, on assumptions about the size of the agent system, and on assumptions about the communication costs. If we assume that an agent migrates only along a preordained migration path, then two mechanisms for locating agents come to mind: firstly, the migration path is searched sequentially, and secondly, the migration path is searched in parallel. CHEN AND LENG (1997) published a third approach. They try to find an agent by guessing its location (see below for the discussion). Since the assumption of a static path stands in contrast to the autonomy propagated by the mobile agent paradigm, we will concentrate on the assumption that the migration path of a mobile agent is not given in advance.

With dynamic paths, three different groups of mechanisms exist: mechanisms using no logging (brute force methods), mechanisms employing logging (either database or path proxies), and mechanisms applying non-deterministic methods. A database can be either centralized or distributed, and paths can be timed (i.e. they are valid only for a limited time) or untimed. For each of the different types of mechanisms implementations exist, which are given at the bottom of Figure 2-2. The energy concept and timed path proxies (in the shadow concept), that have been implemented in Mole, will be introduced in Chapter 4.

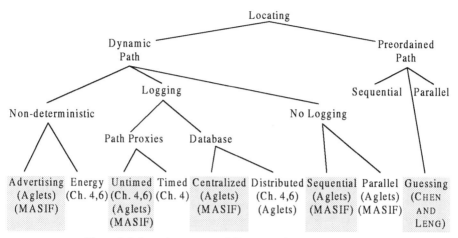

Figure 2-2. Locating agents: different mechanisms.

Let us now examine the different proposed mechanisms.

2.5.1.1 MASIF

According to MILOJICIC ET AL. (1998) MASIF defines an interface named MAF-Finder, which offers methods to locate agents. It allows access to the following location techniques:

1. *Brute force search (dynamic path | no logging | parallel)*. This technique first identifies every agent system in a region, a set of agent systems owned by the same person or organization. Then each system is checked to find the agent.
2. *Logging (dynamic path | logging | path proxies | untimed)*. When an agent leaves an agent system, it leaves on this system a log entry (called mark) that says where it is going. By following the log entries the agent can be located. The log entries are garbage-collected after the agent dies. It is not discussed how this garbage collection is done.
3. *Agent registration (dynamic path | logging | database | centralized)*. Every agent registers its current location in one centralized database. This database can be queried to find the agent.
4. *Agent advertisement (dynamic path | nondeterministic | advertising)*. The agent advertises its location whenever it deems it necessary. To find an agent for which the advertised information is out-of-date, brute force search has to be used.

It is clear that the first technique is no feasible solution for large mobile agent systems. Either the agent can only be found in the own area of authority, or the whole distributed system (in the worst case the Internet) has to be searched. The second technique is comparable with the object proxies discussed in JUL ET AL. (1988) for Emerald. The path concept discussed in Chapter 4 is also similar, but additionally provides the ability to shorten the path to increase the reliability. The main disadvantage of this concept is its low reliability (for details see the fault tolerance discussion in Appendix C.2.1). The third technique places an overhead on the agent migration, delays the agent, since it has to wait for the acknowledgment, and makes the agent migration dependent on the reliability of the network between agent and database. The last approach burdens the agent programmer with the decision when to advertise the agent location. Furthermore, with this technique it is not guaranteed that the agent can be found at all.

2.5.1.2 Aglets Workbench

ARIDOR AND OSHIMA (1998) discuss requirements for a mobile agent infrastructure and present their implementation in the Aglets Workbench. The schemes for locating agents discussed here are very similar to those given in the MASIF. The main differences are:

- the brute force search can be done either sequentially *(dynamic path | no logging | sequential)* or in parallel *(dynamic path | no logging | parallel)*.
- paths created by the logging scheme can be cut short.
- registration can be used with distributed data bases. It is not described how the databases are distributed, but an approach using partitioning could be feasible *(dynamic path | logging | database | distributed)*.
- The advertisement scheme is not part of the Aglets Workbench.

2.5.1.3 Locating Agents with the Help of a Probability Function

In CHEN AND LENG (1997), a mechanism has been proposed that uses the knowledge of an agent's movements to guess its location with the help of a probability function *(preordained path | guessing)*. It assumes a predefined path from which the agent cannot deviate, and tries to compute the current place of the agent using the time interval since the agent left, assuming a binomial distribution of the execution time on each place. This assumption makes the approach unusable for all those applications in which the migration path of the agent is not known in advance. For example, in electronic commerce or in information retrieval scenarios the migration path of the agents depend on information they get while en route. Furthermore, this approach does not guarantee that the agent is found before arriving at its end point, e.g. if the agent leaves every place just before the mechanism guesses this place.

2.5.2 Orphan Detection

Apart from Mole, where the orphan detection mechanisms proposed in Chapter 4 have been implemented, no mobile agent system provides functionality for orphan detection.

2.5.3 Termination

Apart from Mole, which supports termination through the mechanisms described in Chapter 4, only the MASIF standard and the Aglets Workbench discuss termination of agents. In both cases it is expected that the agent's location is known already. It can be assumed that both used the mechanisms for locating agents that they propose. Thus termination is a two-step process, first locating the agent, then sending the termination request to the agent. In contrast to this, the mechanisms proposed in this book combine the locating of the agent and the subsequent termination.

2.5.3.1 MASIF

The MASIF standard provides a method for terminating mobile agents as part of the MAFAgentSystem interface. No further explanation is given.

2.5.3.2 Aglets Workbench

The Aglets Workbench provides one control mechanism that retracts an agent from the place where it is executed. The retraction pulls the aglet from its current place and places it on the place from which this action was requested. The Aglet specification 1.1 (see IBM (1999c)) additionally states that if "[...] the agent is successfully transferred, the receiver must terminate the agent and release any resources consumed by it." Thus a retraction is effectively a termination of a mobile agent, combined with the transfer of its state to the place requesting it.

> *A good model represents a well-balanced abstraction of a real practical situation — not too far from and not too close to the real thing.*
>
> Arto Salomaa, Computation and Automata

3 System and Failure Model

Fault tolerance in distributed computing is a wide area with a substantial body of literature. Until the early 90's, this area was split into many, apparently unrelated, sub-disciplines with distinct terminologies and methodologies. Even terms that are central to the field like "fault", "failure" and "error" had different definitions. These differences hindered the development of a common understanding of even simple failure models. Since then, many attempts towards unification of the field and the terminology failed (see e.g. GÄRTNER (1998A) for details), but the basic terminology at least is common. In this book we follow the terminology defined by JALOTE (1994) with one exception: we use the term *failure model* instead of the term fault model. An introduction to fault tolerance, as far as needed for this book, can be found in Appendix B.

In this chapter our system model and the failure model used for the protocols proposed in this book is introduced. In the later chapters, the system and failure model presented here will be assumed if no other model is explicitly given for that chapter.

3.1 Our System Model

This section describes the system model used throughout this book. A distributed system consists of autonomous nodes that are connected to each other by a communication network.

Each node consists of a processor, private volatile and private stable storage. We assume that each node has access to a correct local hardware clock with a known maximum drift rate. This clock allows the node to manage alarms that e.g. indicate timeouts. The nodes are loosely coupled, do not have shared memory and communicate via message passing.

The communication network is assumed to be fully connected. The delivery of messages is in order, correct, and occurs exactly-once as long as no network failure occurs.

3.2 Our Failure Model

If a component fails in real distributed systems, it is repaired or replaced. In the simplest case this is achieved by rebooting a crashed system. Thus we assume that no failure is permanent, i.e. every encountered failure is transient. This type of failure, proposed by AGUILERA, CHEN AND TOUEG (1998), is an extension of the original crash failure and is called the crash-recovery model.

According to the system model we differentiate between node and network failures. We assume that nodes suffer from crash failures only. The failure causes the node to halt and to lose its internal volatile state. The stable storage survives failures. Communication networks can suffer from crash failures that may cause the network to be partitioned. In the case of a network partition the communication channel between sender and receiver in different partitions fails, but continues to work between participants in the same partition. Node and network failures are detectable, but not distinguishable.

One Ring to rule them all,
One Ring to find them,
One Ring to bring them all
and in the darkness bind them
In the Land of Mordor where the Shadows lie.

J.R.R. Tolkien, The Lord of the Rings

4 Control Mechanisms for Mobile Agents

We have already seen that control mechanisms for mobile agents are needed for mobile agent systems to operate properly. But no work exists yet in the area of mobile agents providing this functionality. Only slowly an understanding of how important this functionality is begins to emerge, and research starts to head in this direction. In this chapter, we will concentrate on different protocols providing control functionality as defined in Chapter 2.4, i.e. functionality for locating agents, for terminating agents and for orphan detection of mobile agents.

First we present the *energy concept*, which supports orphan detection for mobile agents. The underlying idea for this concept is taken from biology, where every organism needs energy to consume the resources of its environment. If it has no more energy, it dies. In this concept every agent is initially provided with some energy. Every action the agent takes, every resource that is used, costs energy. When the energy is used up, the agent is an orphan and can be removed by the system. Locating an agent or terminating it is not possible with this concept.

Then we will discuss the *path concept*, a variant of which is used in the area of distributed systems to track mobile objects. This concept provides functionality for locating agents and for their termination, but offers no orphan detection functionality. Every agent leaves a path in the system, i.e. whenever an agent migrates, information is left behind about the agent's target place. The path can be followed to find the agent, and to interact with it subsequently .

The third concept presented is the *shadow concept* with its variants. This concept supports locating and terminating of mobile agents and furthermore, provides orphan detection functionality. It combines the energy concept and the path concept in a way that leaves the agents most of their autonomy, has low communication costs, and provides excellent fault tolerance. An agent leaves a trail in the system, but in contrast to the trail in the path concept, this trail is cut short at regular intervals. To allow for simple termination of agents, a delegate of the application is left in the system, the shadow. As long as the shadow exists, all dependent agents are allowed to continue their work, i.e. the agents are no longer depending on the availability of the application. Thus no permanent connection between agents and application is needed, i.e. an application is required to run only intermittently to check for results.

Two variants are proposed, namely hierarchical shadows and mobile shadows. Hierarchical shadows expand the original concept in a way that allows agents as well as applications to create shadows. This provides finer control by allowing hierarchical structuring. The shadows created by an agent depend on the same shadow as the agent itself. The mobile shadows variant allows the shadow to move along with the agents to minimize either communication cost or fault sensitivity. Different strategies can be plugged into the shadow, can be combined and can even be changed on the fly. Both variants can be combined to allow even greater flexibility.

This chapter includes a presentation of the different protocols developed for the control of mobile agents. For each of the different protocols we first examine the underlying idea, and then the protocol itself. Fault tolerance discussions and message complexity estimates for each of the presented protocols can be found in Appendix C. A detailed comparison between these protocols and the protocols proposed in Chapter 6 will be presented in Chapter 7.

4.1 The Energy Concept

4.1.1 The Idea

The energy concept provides orphan detection functionality for mobile agents. The mechanism provides neither functionality for locating agents nor for their termination. We start by associating an amount of energy with every agent. In its life an agent consumes resources of the places on which it resides, e.g. CPU time or memory, and uses services provided on a place, for instance a directory service or a local trader. In the energy concept every resource access is combined with a loss of energy for the agent, i.e. the number of an agent's resource accesses is limited (see Figure 4-1).

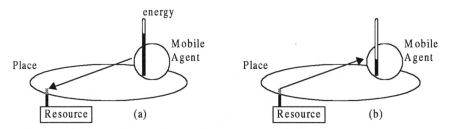

Figure 4-1. Energy concept: energy consumption of services
(a) Service request. (b) Energy is consumed and service provided.

Whenever the energy gets low, the agent can request new energy from its dependency object. The dependency object will normally be the application, but an agent is equally possible as dependency object. When the dependency object no longer exists, the agent gets no more energy. Thus, as soon as the energy of an agent is 0, it is an orphan and can be removed by the system.

With this a simple means exists for determining orphans without remote communication, and with the additional advantage that the activity of an agent, i.e. the use of resources, determines the life span of an agent. Assume that the dependency object's node crashes and the dependency object is lost. After the depending agents' remaining energy has been consumed they are recognized as orphans and automatically removed from the system.

4.1.2   The Protocol

The place on which an agent lives has to decrease the energy of the agent at regular intervals to implement the cost for the consumption of CPU, memory and other resources. The decrease is dependent on the activity of the agent. The agent can be put to sleep via the sleep()-method or awakened via the wake()-method. The sleep()-method removes an agent from the list of living agents and lowers the energy consumption, and the wake()-method adds the agent to the list of living agents and sets the energy consumption to its normal value. If the remaining energy is below a threshold determined by either agent programmer or user, the agent is informed about its precarious situation. If an agent has no energy left, it is an orphan. The system then removes the agent. Every system method called by an agent and every service requested checks if the agent has enough remaining energy . If this is the case, the energy needed for the service is taken from the agent (as illustrated in Figure 4-1) and the system method is called (see Algorithm 4-1).

Regular Intervals:	for each agent
	{
	    if(agent.energy == 0)
	        remove agent;
	    agent.energy -= agent.livingCost ( );
	    if (livingAgents.find (agent) != null)
	        checkLowEnergy (agent);
	}

sleep (agent)	livingAgents.remove (agent); agent.livingCost = place.sleepCost ( );
wake (agent)	livingAgents.add (agent); agent.livingCost = place.livingCost ( );

systemMethod (method, agent)	if (agent.energy < method.cost)
	    throw NotEnoughEnergy;
	agent.energy -= method.cost;
	method.callMethod (agent);

Algorithm 4-1. Energy concept: basic place methods

checkLowEnergy (agent)	if (agent.energy < agent.lowEnergy
	AND agent.refilling == false)
	{
	    agent.energyLow ( );
	    agent.refilling = true;
	}

Algorithm 4-1. Energy concept: basic place methods

The system checks the agent's energy at regular intervals with the method checkLowEnergy(). If the remaining energy is below the threshold, then the agent is informed about its situation by calling the agent method energyLow(). Furthermore the system sets a flag showing that the agent is at the refilling stage. This prevents calling the energyLow()-method again before the agent receives additional energy.

The agent itself has to determine whether its energy lasts long enough to finish its task, or if it needs additional energy. In the second case, as shown in the energyLow()-method of Algorithm 4-2, it sends a request for more energy to its application.

energyLow ( )	[implement policy] Send (home, <"EnergyLow", currentPlace, id>); sleep (this);
receiveEnergy (amount)	[implement policy]; wake (this);

Algorithm 4-2. Energy concept: agent methods

It can then either continue its work or go to sleep, thus minimizing the consumption of energy, while waiting for the answer. In our implementation the agent goes to sleep. As soon as the additional energy is sent to the agent, the system calls the agent method receiveEnergy() to inform it about the change and to wake it up.

When the application receives the request, it can either send additional energy to the agent, i.e. the agent's work is worth the additional resource consumption, or it can deny the request. In the second case no answer and thus no additional communication is necessary, but a negative acknowledgment, a NAK message, can be used to speed up the orphan detection process for the cost of one additional message. The agent can also send additional information, e.g. about its state with its request to allow for a better decision by the application. The example implementation in Algorithm 4-3 grants additional energy for every request.

receiveEnergyRequest:	[a message <"EnergyLow", source, agentId> has arrived] [implement policy] Receive (<"EnergyLow", source, agentId>); Send (from, <agentId, newEnergy>);

Algorithm 4-3. Energy concept: system methods

```
ReceiveEnergyMsg:        [ a message <agentId, newEnergy> has arrived ]
                         Receive ( <agentId, newEnergy> );
                         agent = getAgent ( agentId );
                         agent.energy += newEnergy;
                         if ( agent.energy > agent.lowEnergy )
                         {
                             agent.refilling = false;
                         }
                         agent.receiveEnergy ( );
```

Algorithm 4-3. Energy concept: system methods

When a message containing additional energy is received, the system adds this energy to the agent's energy before calling the agent's receiveEnergy()-method. Additionally the refilling flag is set back to false, if the new energy amount of the agent exceeds the low energy threshold.

The protocol has first been presented in BAUMANN (1997) and has been implemented by JOCHUM (1997).

4.1.3 Discussion

The advantages of the energy concept are obvious. All information to check if an agent is an orphan is available locally; no additional communication is necessary to determine if an agent is an orphan (see discussion in Appendix C.1). Furthermore, only a well-defined amount of resources can be consumed by an agent before it has to contact the dependency object, i.e. the worst-case cost for an agent's activities is known beforehand. While the energy concept clearly has strong similarities to a currency concept, it has one major difference. If a place steals money from each agent that visits it, this stolen money can be used e.g. to buy something. If a place steals energy, the agent might need to refill its energy sooner, but the stolen energy cannot be used by the place or the place's owner.

4.2 The Path Concept

The path concept provides functionality for locating agents and for their termination. The mechanism does not provide orphan detection functionality for mobile agents, i.e. we use no dependency object for the path concept. The idea of paths is a well-known technique in the area of distributed systems (e.g. discussed in FOWLER (1985)), used for locating distributed objects. The path is a distributed structure pointing towards the object in question, and has to be followed to reach the object. The single elements of the path, i.e. the data structures on a node, are called proxies. Paths have been discussed for the object-based distributed system Emerald in BLACK ET AL. (1987) and in JUL ET AL. (1988), or the object-oriented distributed system Arjuna. An introduction to Arjuna can be found in PARRINGTON ET

AL. (1995), and CAUGHEY AND SHRIVASTAVA (1995) discuss the details of object mobility in Arjuna. Paths are used for tracking mobile users in AWERBUCH AND PELEG (1995), for the forwarding of IP packets in the Mobile Host Routing Protocol (presented in JOHNSON (1994)), and in the area of distributed garbage collection, e.g. for the Stub-Scion-Pair chains as proposed in SHAPIRO, DICKMAN AND PLAINFOSSÉ (1992A).

4.2.1 The Idea

An agent moves through a mobile agent system in an unforeseeable manner, i.e. normally no predictions can be made about its location at a certain time. But if every agent leaves its new location on the old place when it migrates, i.e. leaves a proxy, then a path of proxies is created. This path of proxies can be followed if the place where the agent has been created, called the anchor place, is known. This path ultimately leads to the agent place, i.e. the place on which the agent resides currently (see Figure 4-2). The main problems of this approach are the house keeping, i.e. how the proxies can be removed when the path is no longer valid, and the dependence on the availability of a high number of participants, the proxy nodes.

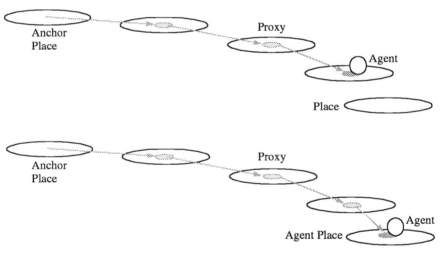

Figure 4-2. Path concept: creating the path upon migration

4.2.2 The Protocol

The path can be created by creating a proxy pointing to the destination place of an agent when it leaves. In Algorithm 4-4 the system methods for an agent arriving and leaving a place are given. At arrival nothing has to be done, but upon leaving a new proxy is added to the path of proxies. This path proxy contains the agent id and the target of the migration.

OnArrival:	[an *agent* has arrived] Receive (agent); agentList.add (agent);
onLeaving:	[*agent* leaves towards *target*] agentList.remove (agent); pathProxyList.add (new PathProxy (agent.id, target)); Send (target, <agent>);

Algorithm 4-4. Path concept: creating a trail

Finding agents can be divided into two simple steps. First we have to check if the agent is on the current place. If it is not on the current place, and no proxy exists for this agent, then a message containing a *find* request is sent to the anchor place. If a proxy exists, a request is sent to the target place stored in the proxy containing the searching place and the agent id, thus initiating a search for the agent. The receiving place determines if the agent is on that place. If that is the case it sends the information back to the original searching place. If a proxy exists, the request is sent onward, until the agent is found at the end of the path (see Algorithm 4-5).

find (agentId)	if (agentList.find (agentId) != null)
	    return (currentPlace);
	pathProxy = pathProxyList.find (agentId);
	if (pathProxy != null)
	{
	    target = pathProxy.target;
	    Send (target, <"Find", currentPlace, agentId>);
	}
	else
	    return (notFoundError);

ReceiveFind:	[a message <"Find", searcher, agentId> has arrived]
	Receive (<"Find", searcher, agentId>);
	if (agentList.find (agentId) != null)
	    send (searcher, <"Found", currentPlace, agentId>);
	if (pathProxyList.find (agentId) != null)
	    Send (pathProxy.target, <"Find", searcher, agentId>);
	else
	    Send (searcher, <"NotFoundError", agentId>);

ReceiveFound:	[a message <"Found", from, agentId> has arrived] Receive (<"Found", from, agentId>); return(from);
ReceiveError:	[a message <"NotFoundError", agentId> has arrived] Receive (<"NotFoundError", agentId>); return (notFoundError);

Algorithm 4-5. Path concept: methods for finding agents

If no proxy is found on a place, then an error message is sent back to the original requesting place. By sending a termination request together with the find request the agent can be terminated without additional messages.

The protocol has first been discussed in BAUMANN (1997).

4.2.2.1 Shortening the Path

We will now examine a variant of the path concept that allows a decrease in the number of path proxies whenever a search for an agent is successful. If the information about the location of the agent is sent to the anchor place, the path can be shortened by setting the target of the proxy at the anchor place to the new place. This way the information can be updated without additional communication. The intermediate proxies are now useless and can be removed. A "shortenPath"-request is sent along the old path, containing the beginning of the new path. A place receiving this request examines if it contains the proxy representing the beginning of the new path. If this is the case, then the superfluous old path segment is removed. Otherwise, it sends the request onward and removes the local proxy (see Algorithm 4-6).

ReceiveFound:	[a message <"Found", from, agentId> has arrived]
	Receive (<"Found", from, agentId>);
	pathProxy = pathProxyList.find (agentId);
	Send (pathProxy.target, <"ShortenPath", from, agentId>);
	pathProxy.target = from;
	return (from);

ReceiveError:	[a message <"NotFoundError", agentId> has arrived] Receive (<"NotFoundError", agentId>); Send (pathProxy.target, <"ShortenPath", from, agentId>); return (notFoundError);

ShortenPath:	[a message <"ShortenPath", target, agentId> has arrived]
	Receive (<"ShortenPath", target, agentId>);
	pathProxy = pathProxyList.find (agentId);
	if (target != this AND pathProxy != null)
	{
	    nextProxy = pathProxy.target;
	    Send (nextProxy, <"ShortenPath", target, agentId>);
	    pathProxyList.remove (pathProxy);
	}

Algorithm 4-6. Path concept: shortening the path

Additionally, if the agent moves back to a place it visited before, the now circular path can be cut short. Also, if an error is received at the inquiring site, then the path is broken and can be removed. Both can be done with the same "shortenPath"-request. The problem of the variant is that it is unpredictable when the path will be cut short, i.e. when a search will be initiated. In the worst case, i.e. if no search is initiated at all, the path is never cut short.

4.2.3 Discussion

The path concept allows the agents to roam the network without having to contact their home location. In contrast to the energy concept, no additional communication cost is introduced by establishing the paths. The disadvantages result from the path not being limited in length. The communication cost to find an agent can be arbitrarily high, directly dependent on the length of the path. Furthermore, the path depends on all visited systems being reachable (see the discussion in Appendix C). If only one of the intermediate systems is not reachable, the agent cannot be found. Thus the longer the path the worse is the availability.

4.3 The Shadow Protocol

Now we describe the shadow protocol with all its variants and optimizations. The shadow protocol provides functionality for locating agents, for their termination and for orphan detection. In this concept every agent has an associated shadow (which might be shared with other agents of the same application), i.e. the shadow is the dependency object. Thus, the agent is an orphan when the shadow no longer exists. We start with the basic protocol, examine the hierarchical and mobile shadows, discuss their combination and show possible optimizations.

4.3.1 The Basic Protocol

The shadow concept is a combination of variants of the energy concept and the path concept, combining the positive properties of each concept while minimizing the negative properties. We start with the shadows themselves, then add the variation of the energy concept, and finally include a path concept variant.

4.3.1.1 The Idea

In the shadow concept each application creates one or more dependency objects called *shadows*, a data structure on a place. The place on which the shadow is created, does not necessarily have to be situated on the same host on which the creating application runs. Each agent created by the application depends on such a shadow (Figure 4-3), and not on the application itself. Thus the agents started by an application no longer have to contact the application. This allows the application to execute on a system not permanently connected to the network, or to run the application only intermittently.

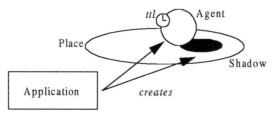

Figure 4-3. Shadows: the creation of a shadow

At regular intervals, called *time to live* or *ttl*, the system checks for each agent whether the associated shadow still exists; the agent enters the *check phase* until a new time quantum is received (Figure 4-4). An agent in the check phase is not allowed to migrate. This differs from the energy concept in employing a time interval, instead of resource consumption, as the limiting factor.

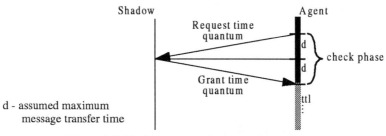

Figure 4-4. Shadows: requesting a new time quantum

If the shadow does no longer exist, e.g. because the application removed it, the agent is, according to the definition, an orphan. This is detected after the allotted time quantum has been used up. If a place on which a shadow is located cannot be reached, the agent tries to contact the place periodically (Figure 4-5). After *n* unsuccessful attempts the protocol assumes that the node hosting the place has crashed.

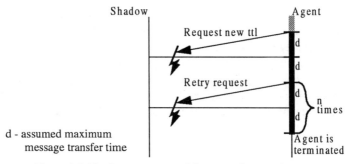

Figure 4-5. Shadows: unsuccessful request for new time quantum

The protocol now implies that the shadow is lost, the agent is an orphan and can be removed from the system. If the place cannot be reached because its node has crashed, then this behaviour is correct. If the place cannot be reached because a network partition prevented communication, then the agent has been terminated incorrectly. But the shadow concludes correctly that the agent has been terminated and removes it from its list of dependants. This behaviour guarantees correct information in the shadow even in the presence of network partitions.

The disadvantage of this approach is that regardless of what an agent does, it has to connect to its shadow's place at regular intervals. If this contact is not possible, e.g. because the network is partitioned, then the agent is removed even if the shadow would have returned a new time quantum. The advantage is that we have a worst-case time bound for the termination of agents through removing the shadows, namely $ttl + 2(n+1)d$, with d as the assumed maximum message transfer time and ttl as the time quantum allotted to the agent. If an agent has not contacted the shadow after this worst-case time bound, then the shadow knows that the agent has terminated.

According to our agent model discussed in Chapter 2.3 agents are able to create child agents. Thus, if an agent creates a new agent, the system assigns the shadow of the creating agent and the remaining ttl of the creating agent to this new agent (Figure 4-6). It is important that a newly created agent gets only the remaining ttl of the creating agent, and not the full ttl. If the latter would be the case, then an agent could live infinitely long by instantiating a copy of itself with full ttl shortly before its ttl drops to 0.

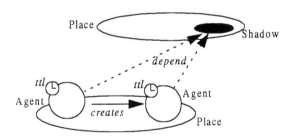

Figure 4-6. Shadows: creating a new agent

It is clear that the protocol described so far is a variant of the energy concept with the shadow as the dependency object and time instead of energy as the limiting factor. Thus the protocol allows only orphan detection. By removing a shadow all dependent agents are declared to be orphans, and after the worst-case time bound $ttl + 2(n+1)d$ has passed, it is guaranteed that all agents have been detected by the orphan detection and have been removed by the sysem.

By adding a variant of the path concept to this protocol (see Chapter 4.2), we also allow termination. In principle, the unmodified path concept could be used, but by using the additional information about the agent's ttl, no additional communication is needed to remove the superfluous path segments. How is this done? An agent contacts its shadow when its *ttl* is 0. With this communication, the shadow can update its information about the place on which the agent resides, and the old path is no longer needed. By keeping the *ttl* with every agent proxy, it can be determined locally, i.e. without additional communication, whether the agent proxy is still needed as part of a current path (see Figure 4-7). Even if the path is broken, e.g. because a node crashed, the worst-case time until the agent is reachable again is the *ttl*, because after that time it will have contacted the shadow again.

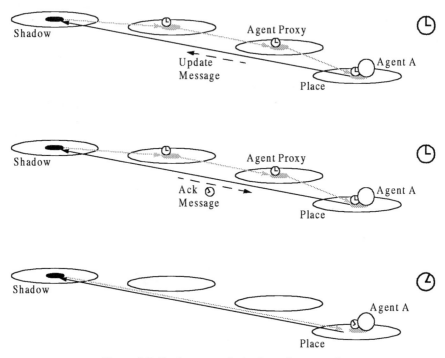

Figure 4-7. Shadows: regular update of proxy paths

4.3.1.2 The Protocol

The following functionality has been omitted in the protocol discussion, because while in principle simple, it obscures the view on the interesting parts of the protocol:

- limiting the path length. This is done by counting the number of hops.
- parallel requests, e.g. for locating agents. This is done by using globally unique identifiers to identify request / answer pairs.
- subtracting the migration time from the *ttl* of an agent.

As before, we discuss the different parts separately. The protocol deviates from the idea sketched above in so far as all path proxies of different agents belonging to the same shadow are put in one object, the agent proxy.

Agent Migration. When an agent arrives on a place, an agent proxy is created if it does not already exist, with the agent's *ttl*, its id and its shadow's id (Algorithm 4-7). When an agent wants to leave a place, the agent's *ttl* is checked and migration is only allowed if *ttl* is greater than 0. If this is not the case, an exception is thrown; this is done to prevent a migration while the agent is in the check phase. If migration is allowed, a reference to the target place is entered into the agent proxy to create a new path segment and a timer with the remaining *ttl* of the agent, the proxy-time-out, is started to allow removal of the path when it is no longer required.

The place on which the agent resides decrements the *ttl* of the agent at regular intervals, which are much shorter than the *ttl*. As soon as the *ttl* of the agent is 0, a message is sent back to the shadow's place, containing the id of the agent and the id of the shadow. At the same time a timer is started with the check-phase-time-out, and the agent enters the *check phase*. As a security measure the lesser of the agent-specific and a place-specific time-out is chosen for this time-out.

OnArrival:	[an *agent* has arrived]
	Receive (agent);
	agentproxy = proxyList.find (agent.shadowId);
	if (agentproxy == null)
	{
	    agentproxy = new AgentProxy (agent.id, agent.timeToLive,
	                                        agent.shadowHome,
	                                        currentPlace);
	    proxyList.add (agentproxy);
	}
	else
	    agentproxy.add (agent.agentId, agent.timeToLive);
	agent.proxy = agentproxy;
	agentList.add (agent);
	agent.start ( );

OnLeaving:	[*agent* leaves towards *target*]
	if (agent.timeToLive > 0)
	{
	    agentList.remove (agent);
	    agent.proxy.setTarget (agent.id, target);
	    startTimer (agent.timeToLive + agent.timeOut,
	                agent.proxy, agent.id);
	    Send (target, <agent>);
	}
	else
	    Throw (CheckPhaseException);

Algorithm 4-7. Shadows: system methods

Regular Intervals:	for each agent
	{
	    agent.timeToLive - -;
	    if (agent.timeToLive == 0)
	    {
	        Send (agent.shadowHome,
	                <"Chk", currentPlace, agent.shadowId, agent.id>);
	        startTimer (min (localTimeOut, agent.timeOut),
	                      agent.proxy, agent);
	    }
	}

Algorithm 4-7. Shadows: system methods

Check Phase. The check message is received by the home place of the shadow. First the shadow stops a timer for the ttl-time-out, that had been started by this method when the *ttl* was sent the last time. This timer is used to detect agents that have terminated (see below and Algorithm 4-10). The shadow determines the new *ttl* for the agent, which is then sent back if greater than 0. As soon as the message is received on the place where the agent resides, the timer for the check-phase-time-out is stopped, and the agent's *ttl* and the *ttl* of the agent proxy is set (Algorithm 4-8). This ends the check phase and the agent is allowed to migrate again.

ReceiveCheck:	[a message <"Chk", from, shadowId, agentId> has arrived]
	Receive (<"Chk", currentPlace, agent.shadowId, agent.id>);
	shadow = shadowList.find (shadowId);
	timeToLive = shadow.timeToLive (from, agentId);
	if (timeToLive > 0)
	{
	    shadow.stopTimer (agentId);
	    shadow.startTimer (shadow.getTimeOut (agentId)
	                         + timeToLive, shadow, agentId);
	    sendAllowance (from,
	                      <"Allowance", agentId, timeToLive>);
	}

ReceiveAllowance:	[a message <"Allowance", agentId, timeToLive> has arrived]
	Receive (<"Allowance", agentId, timeToLive>);
	stopTimer (agentId);
	agent = agentList.findAgent (agentId);
	agent.timeToLive = timeToLive;
	agent.proxy.setTTL (timeToLive);

Algorithm 4-8. Shadows: the check phase

The shadow can decide for each request whether it should be answered by sending a new grant, and how long the new *ttl* sent back to the agent should be. A simple example of how the shadow determines the new *ttl* for an agent is shown in Algorithm 4-9. Here for all agents the same *ttl* is returned. At the same time the location information is updated. First the shadow's list of agents is searched for an entry. If none is found, then this agent must have been created by a dependent agent and contacts the shadow for the first time; an entry is created with the reported location of the agent. If the entry already exists, then the place on which the agent resides is updated in the entry. Now the new *ttl* is returned. The shadow is also called if the system has detected, via the allowance-time-out (see below), that an agent has been terminated. Here the related entry is removed from the list.

timeToLive (from, agentId)	[implement policy]
	agentEntry = listOfProxies.find (agentId);
	if (agentEntry != null)
	    agentEntry.target = from;
	else
	{
	    timeToLive = computeTimeToLive(agentId);
	    agentEntry = new AgentEntry (from, agentId,
	                                        timeToLive);
	    listOfProxies.add (agentEntry);
	}
	return agentEntry.timeToLive;

remove (agentId)	[implement policy] agentEntry = listOfProxies.find (agentId); agentEntry.remove (agentId);

Algorithm 4-9. Shadows: methods in the shadow object

Time-outs. Three different time-outs can occur in the basic protocol (see Algorithm 4-10). These are the time-out for the agent proxies (the proxy-time-out, see Algorithm 4-7), the time-out in the check phase (the check-phase-time-out, see Algorithm 4-7), and the time-out if an agent did not contact the shadow for the sum of *ttl* and check phase time-out (the allowance-time-out, see Algorithm 4-8). The time-out for the agent proxies is the result of the timer started when the agent migrates. It signals that in the meantime the agent has to have contacted its shadow and updated the path information, i.e. this part of the path is useless and can be removed. If the entry was the last entry in the agent proxy, then the agent proxy is removed also (action **ProxyPathTimeOut**). The time-out in the check-phase occurs if no grant for a new *ttl* is received in time. The agent is then declared an orphan and is removed (action **AllowanceTimeOut**). The last time-out occurs if an agent has not contacted its shadow for the worst-case time bound $ttl + 2(n+1)d$. This happens either because it has terminated before its *ttl* was used up, or because it wasn't able to reach the shadow in time to receive another grant and has been removed by the system, e.g. because of a network partition. In both cases the agent no longer exists; the shadow method remove() presented in Algorithm 4-9 is called to react to this, i.e. to remove the agent's entry (action **AgentRequestTimeOut**). A more sophisticated implementation of the shadow could, for example, initiate the start of another agent with the same goals.

ProxyPathTimeOut:	[the timer triggered a <timer, agentproxy, agentId> message] Receive (<timer, agentproxy, agentId>); agentproxy.remove (agentId); if (agentproxy.entries ( ) == 0) proxyList.remove (agentproxy);
AllowanceTimeOut:	[the timer triggered a <timer, agentproxy, agent> message] [implement policy] Receive (<timer, agentproxy, agent>); agent.stop ( ); agentList.remove (agent); agentproxy.remove (agentId); if (agentproxy.entries ( ) == 0) proxyList.remove (agentproxy);
AgentRequestTimeOut:	[the timer triggered a <timer, shadow, agentId> message] Receive (<timer, shadow, agentId>); shadow.remove (agentId);

Algorithm 4-10. Shadows: reaction to time-outs

Locating Agents. Before an agent can be terminated, it has to be found. This can be done with the help of the path information stored in the agent proxies (see Algorithm 4-11). If the searched agent is on the same place as the initiator, then it is found by looking it up in the list of agents on the local place. If it is not there, then the agent proxy is identified and a *find* message is sent to the target place found in it. If no agent proxy exists for it, an error is returned. As soon as the *find* message is received on the target place, the local list of agents is examined, and if the agent is found, a success message is sent back to the inquirer. If it is not found, the list of agent proxies is searched, and if a path entry for the agent is found, the request is sent onward. If not, an error is sent back. This is repeated until the agent is found or the path ends.

find (agentId)	if (agentList.find (agentId) != null)
	    return (currentPlace);
	for each shadow in shadowList
	    if (agentEntry = shadow.find (agentId) != null)
	        break;
	if (agentEntry != null)
	{
	    target = agentEntry.target (agentId);
	    Send (target, <"Find", currentPlace, agentId>);
	}
	else
	    return (notFoundError);

Algorithm 4-11. Shadows: locating agents

ReceiveFind:	[a message <"Find", searcher, agentId> has arrived]
	Receive (<"Find", searcher, agentId>);
	if (agentList.find (agentId) != null)
	    Send (searcher, <"Found", currentPlace, agentId>);
	else
	{
	    if (agentProxy = placeProxyList.find (agentId) != null)
	    {
	        target = agentProxy.target (agentId);
	        Send (target, <"Find", searcher, agentId>);
	    }
	    else
	        Send (searcher, <"NotFoundError", agentId>);
	}

ReceiveFound:	[a message <"Found", from, agentId> has arrived] Receive (<"Found", from, agentId>); return (from);
ReceiveError:	[a message <"NotFoundError", agentId> has arrived] Receive (<"NotFoundError", agentId>); return(notFoundError);

Algorithm 4-11. Shadows: locating agents

One problem is not addressed in Algorithm 4-11: if the agent requests a new *ttl* while a request is under way, then the path proxies might already have been removed and the request lost. Thus the shadow stores the *find* request, and if the agent contacts the shadow before the *find* message is answered, the new location of the agent is returned. A possible later answer to the original *find* message is ignored.

The basic protocol has first been presented by BAUMANN (1997), and has been implemented by ZEPF (1996).

4.3.2 Hierarchical Shadows

4.3.2.1 The Idea

Many applications for mobile agents try to solve problems that can be partitioned into smaller problems. These smaller problems could be solved individually by different subgroups of agents. Example scenarios in which such partitioning is useful have been given in BAUMANN AND RADOUNIKLIS (1997). The basic protocol does not model a hierarchical structuring to support the division of a problem; grouping of agents is only done at the application level. The alleviation of this disadvantage is the concept of hierarchical shadows (see Figure 4-8).

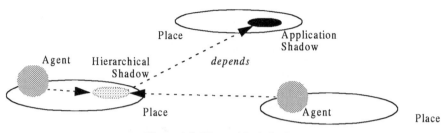

Figure 4-8. Hierarchical shadows

A hierarchical shadow has the same functionality as the application shadow presented in the basic protocol, but depends on another shadow in the same way as an agent does. Furthermore, it can be created by either application or agent (see Figure 4-9). A hierarchical shadow is owned by its dependency object, i.e. either application or agent and can either be removed through the owner's intervention.

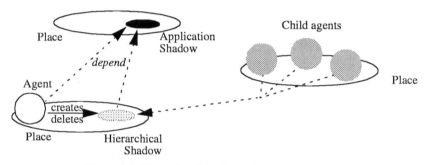

Figure 4-9. Hierarchical shadows: fine-grained control

This allows hierarchically structured relationships inside the agent system without relaxing the control on any level. If an agent owning a hierarchical shadow creates child agents, e.g. for a search in a distributed tree-structured source of information, and associates these child agents with the hierarchical shadow, all agents dependent of this shadow can be terminated by the owning agent as soon as this agent decides they are no longer needed. Furthermore, the functionality of the basic protocol ensures that if the application shadow is removed, then subsequently all hierarchical shadows depending on this shadow and thus all their agents are removed as well.

Without this mechanism, all of the child agents would belong to the one shadow owned by the application, and terminating exactly the now needless agents would be a tedious chore. With hierarchical shadows, the agent creates first a hierarchical shadow, and subsequently all child agents will depend on this shadow. If later it wants to terminate its child agents, it simply removes the hierarchical shadow instead of terminating every child agent explicitly.

4.3.2.2 The Protocol

In this section we only discuss the changes and extensions to the basic protocol necessary to implement the hierarchical shadows. In the hierarchical shadow concept, a place does not only have to check all agents at regular intervals, but hierarchical shadows residing on it as well. Algorithm 4-12 contains the addition to the method called at regular intervals to ensure this. The *ttl* of every hierarchical shadow is decremented at regular intervals. As soon as it drops to 0 a message is sent to the parent shadow's place and a timer is started. This marks the beginning of the hierarchical shadow's check phase.

Regular Intervals:	[agent related part stays the same]
	for each hShadow
	{
	    hShadow.timeToLive - -;
	    if (hShadow.timeToLive == 0)
	    {
	        Send (hShadow.parentShadowHome,
	            <"Chk", currentPlace,
	                hshadow.parentShadowId,
	                hshadow.hShadowId>);
	        startTimer (min (localTimeOut, hShadow.timeOut),
	                hShadow);
	    }
	}

Algorithm 4-12. Hierarchical shadows: extended methods for regular intervals

Shadow Check Phase. The check message is received by the place on which the hierarchical shadow's parent shadow resides. The parent shadow is identified and the timer associated with this hierarchical shadow, i.e. the timer started when the last *ttl* was sent, is stopped. The parent shadow determines the new *ttl* for the child shadow, the timer is started anew and the new *ttl* is sent back to the child shadow. As soon as the new *ttl* is received by the place on which the agent resides, the timer started in Algorithm 4-12 is stopped, and the shadow's *ttl* is set to the new value. Thus ends the check phase of the shadow.

ReceiveShadowCheck:	[a message <"Chk", from, shadowId, hShadowId> has arrived]
	shadow = shadowList.find (shadowId);
	shadow.stopTimer (hShadowId);
	timeToLive = shadow.timeToLive (hShadowId);
	if (timeToLive > 0)
	{
	    Send (from, <"Allowance", hShadowId, timeToLive>);
	    shadow.startTimer (shadow.getTimeOut (hShadowId)
	                    + timeToLive, shadow, hShadowId);
	}

Algorithm 4-13. Hierarchical shadows: the shadow's check phase

ReceiveShadowAllowance:	[a message <"Allowance", shadowId, timeToLive> has arrived]
	Receive (<"Allowance", shadowId, timeToLive>);
	stopTimer (shadowId);
	shadow = shadowList.findShadow (shadowId);
	shadow.timeToLive = timeToLive;

Algorithm 4-13. Hierarchical shadows: the shadow's check phase

In Algorithm 4-14 the analogue to the simple mechanism presented in Algorithm 4-8 is shown, i.e. every child shadow requesting a new *ttl* gets the same standard *ttl* back. If the shadow requesting the new *ttl* is not yet entered in the list of dependent shadows, it is added to it. This happens for example, if an agent associated with the shadow creates a new hierarchical shadow.

timeToLive
(from, shadowId)
	[implement policy]
	subShadowEntry = listOfSubShadows.find (shadowId);
	if (subShadowEntry != null)
	    subShadowEntry.target = from;
	else
	{
	    subShadowEntry = new SubShadowEntry
	                       (from, shadowId, timeToLive);
	    listOfSubShadows.add (subShadowEntry);
	}
	return subShadowEntry.timeToLive;

remove (shadowId)	[implement policy] subShadowEntry = listOfSubShadows.find (shadowId); listOfSubShadows.remove (subShadowEntry);

Algorithm 4-14. Hierarchical shadows: additional shadow methods

Time-Outs. Additionally to the time-outs of the basic protocol, two time-outs are needed for the hierarchical shadows. The first one assures that a hierarchical shadow is removed if it does not receive a new *ttl* (action **ShadowAllowanceTimeOut**), the other ensures accurate information in the parent shadow by signalling that a child shadow has not contacted the parent shadow for so long a time that the child shadow has to have been removed by the system (action **ShadowRequestTimeOut**).

ShadowAllowanceTimeOut:	[the timer triggered a <timer, hShadow> message] [implement policy] Receive (<timer, hShadow>); shadowList.remove (hShadow);
ShadowRequestTimeOut:	[the timer triggered a <timer, shadow, hShadowId> message] Receive (<timer, shadow, hShadowId>); shadow.remove (hShadowId);

Algorithm 4-15. Hierarchical shadows: reaction to time-outs

The protocol for hierarchical shadows been has been implemented by ZEPF (1996).

4.3.2.3 Locating Agents

The Idea. The tree structure created by the hierarchical shadows makes finding of agents a little bit more complicated than in the basic protocol. The main difference is that the application shadow does no longer know all of the agents dependent on it. A shadow knows only those agents that are directly depending on it. Thus when an agent is searched every shadow has to send requests to all of its dependent shadows requesting the location of this agent until the agent is found. When the agent is found, the positive response is sent at once. When a shadow cannot find an agent, it reports a negative result to its parent shadow. A shadow can report this result only, if the agent in question does not directly depend on it, and if all child shadows have already reported negative results. Thus the number of unanswered requests to child shadows has to be counted (see the variable *count* in Figure 4-10).

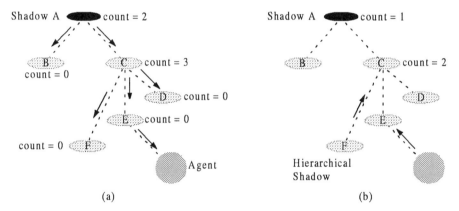

Figure 4-10. Hierarchical shadows: locating an agent
(a) Sending the request. (b) Answering the request.

In Figure 4-10a a request is sent from shadow A along a hierarchy of shadows. In Figure 4-10b it has received a negative answer from shadow B, i.e. the number of open requests is 1, and shadow C has already received a negative answer from D. Shortly C will receive a positive result from E and send it to A.

The Protocol. We implement two stages for finding the agents, one in which the request is distributed to the child shadows, and a second in which all answers are gathered and reported to the next higher level in the hierarchy of shadows. As before the protocol presented here is slightly simplified and does not allow parallel requests. In reality every request in the first stage is assigned a globally unique identifier to allow the correct association of the answers in the second stage.

The first stage starts when the application shadow is asked for the location of an agent. First it is checked if the agent resides on the current place. If it is not found there, then the shadow checks its list of agent proxies. If the agent is found in the list, then the search functionality of the basic protocol is used to follow the proxy path. If this is not the case, then a *find* request is sent to all child shadows, the number of expected answers, i.e. the number of child shadows, is stored for later use and a timer is started to detect shadows that do not answer. An error is returned only if no child shadows exist (see Algorithm 4-16).

When subsequently a *find* request is received by one of the child shadows, nearly the same procedure as in the application shadow starts. First it is checked if the agent is on the current place, then the list of agent proxies is searched. If both searches do not produce a positive result, the shadow sends *find* requests to its child shadows. It stores the number of requests and starts a timer. An error is returned if the agent cannot be found directly and no child shadows exist.

This way the request is sent through the whole tree of hierarchical shadows. By asking the child shadows to send the results to the current place instead of the application shadow it is guaranteed that a negative answer can be given as well as a positive one.

find (shadowId, agentId)	if (agentList.find (agentId) != null)
	    return (currentPlace);
	shadow = shadowList.find (shadowId);
	if (shadow == null)
	    return (notFoundError);
	agentEntry = shadow.find (agentId);
	if (agentEntry != null)
	{
	    target = agentEntry.target;
	    Send (target, <"Find", currentPlace, agentId>);
	}
	else
	    if (listOfSubShadows.isEmpty ( ) == true)
	        return (notFoundError);
	    else
	    {
	        for each subShadowEntry in listOfSubShadows
	            Send (subShadowEntry.target ( ),
	                <"Find", currentPlace,
	                subShadowEntry.shadowId, agentId>);
	        this.answers.count = listOfSubShadows.numEntries ( );
	        startTimer (shadowId, agentId);
	    }

Algorithm 4-16. Hierarchical shadows: propagating a *find* request

```
ReceiveFind:              [ a message <"Find", searcher, shadowId, agentId> has arrived ]
                          Receive ( <"Find", currentPlace, shadowId, agentId> );
                          if ( agentList.find ( agentId ) != null )
                              Send (   searcher,
                                       <"Found", currentPlace, shadowId, agentId> );
                          hShadow = shadowList.find ( shadowId );
                          if ( hShadow == null )
                              Send ( searcher, <"NotFoundError", shadowId, agentId> );
                          agentEntry = hShadow.find (agentId);
                          if ( agentEntry != null )
                              Send ( agentEntry.target,
                                       <"Find", currentPlace, agentId> );
                          else
                              if ( listOfSubShadows.isEmpty ( ) == true )
                              Send ( searcher, <"NotFoundError", shadowId, agentId> );
                              else
                              {
                                  for each subShadowEntry in listOfHShadows
                                      Send (   subShadowEntry.target,
                                               <"Find", currentPlace,
                                               subShadowEntry.shadowId, agentId> );
                                  this.answers.count = listOfSubShadows.numEntries ( );
                                  this.answers.searcher = searcher;
                                  startTimer ( shadowId, agentId );
                              }
```

Algorithm 4-16. Hierarchical shadows: propagating a *find* request

Two answers are possible to the *find* requests, either signalling that the agent has been found or that no shadow in the branch, of which the sender is the root, was able to find the agent (see Algorithm 4-17). If the agent has been found, the associated shadow is identified, the associated timer is stopped (see below) and the count of answers is set to 0. This ensures that no negative answer can be generated later. If the shadow is the application shadow, then the answer is simply returned, otherwise a message is sent to the parent shadow.

If an error is received, then again the shadow is identified, and the number of answers already received is checked. If it is 0, then the agent has already been found and this message is ignored. Otherwise the count is decremented. If the value just dropped to 0, then the timer is stopped, and either the answer is returned if the shadow is the application shadow, or sent onward to the parent shadow.

```
ReceiveFound:        [ a message <"Found", place, shadowId, agentId> has arrived ]
                     Receive ( <"Found", place, shadowId, agentId> );
                     stopTimer ( shadowId, agentId );
                     shadow = ListOfShadows.find ( shadowId );
                     shadow.answers.count = 0;
                     if ( shadow.appShadow == null )
                         return ( place );
                     else
                         Send (   shadow.answers.searcher,
                                  <"Found", place, shadowId, agentId> );

ReceiveError:        [ a message <"NotFoundError", shadowId, agentId> arrived ]
                     Receive ( <"NotFoundError", shadowId, agentId> );
                     shadow = ListOfShadows.find ( shadowId );
                     if ( shadow.answers.count != 0 )
                     {
                         shadow.answers.count --;
                         if ( shadow.answers.count == 0 )
                         {
                             stopTimer ( shadowId, agentId );
                             if ( shadow.appShadow == null )
                                 return ( notFoundError );
                             else
                                 Send (   shadow.answers.searcher,
                                          <"NotFoundError", shadowId, agentId> );
                         }
                     }
```

Algorithm 4-17. Hierarchical shadows: collecting the answers for a *find* request

A timer is started when the find request is sent to the child shadows of a shadow. If this timer signals, then at least one of these shadows was not able to give a negative answer in time. The count of answers is set to 0 to suppress possible later answers,

```
OnTimer:             [ the timer triggered a <timer, shadowId, agentId> message ]
                     Receive ( <timer, shadowId, agentId> );
                     shadow = ListOfShadows.find ( shadowId );
                     shadow.answers.count = 0;
                     if ( shadow.appShadow == null )
                         return ( notFoundError );
                     else
                         Send (   shadow.answers.searcher,
                                  <"NotFoundError", shadowId, agentId> );
```

Algorithm 4-18. Hierarchical shadows: reaction to time-outs when locating agents

the shadow is examined, and either an answer is returned to the caller if this shadow is the application shadow, or a negative answer sent to the parent shadow.

The simple version of the protocol for locating agents shown here has one advantage: it is straightforward to discuss. But it has also some disadvantages that have to be examined. The first one is that multiple requests are not supported. This can be alleviated by using globally unique identifiers. The second disadvantage is that the time-out between the different hierarchy levels is not negotiated. This can be changed by sending the time-out as a parameter with the request, thus allowing for adjustment of the time-outs. The third disadvantage of this version is that, if a new branch is added after a request is started, e.g. because an agent has created a new hierarchical shadow, this new branch is not included in the search. By sending an additional request to this shadow with a shorter time-out it can be included in the search. To sum up this discussion, while the simplified protocol presented here has some drawbacks, it has the same properties regarding message complexity and fault tolerance as the more sophisticated variant that alleviates the disadvantages; thus we will use this variant for the discussion of message complexity and fault tolerance in Appendix C.

4.3.3 Mobile Shadows

The underlying assumption regarding the behaviour of mobile agents in designing the basic protocol and the hierarchical shadows was, that agents do not move in concert from one geographical region to the next. But let us assume the following scenario: an application running in Berlin starts agents searching distributed databases. These agents migrate to the United States and start searching there. Now every request for a new *ttl* of every agent has to be sent from the US to Europe, and every grant has to be sent back (see Figure 4-11).

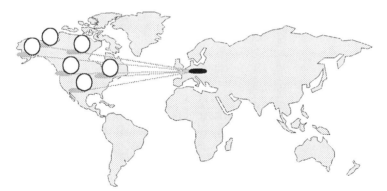

*Figure 4-11. Shadows: high communication costs
due to the shadow's non-mobility*

It is clear that this form of interaction has high communication costs. As soon as we assume a form of agent migration in which a number of agents moves together from region to region, it is advantageous if the shadow follows the agents, i.e. places itself in a location where for example the communication costs are lower.

With mobile shadows in the above scenario, the shadow could place itself somewhere in the US to interact with its dependent agents, and leave only a shadow proxy at its home place (Figure 4-12). When the agents move on, the shadow can follow again.

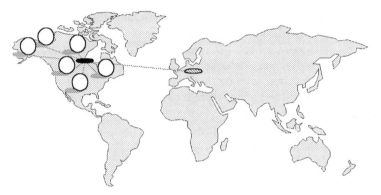

Figure 4-12. Mobile shadows: the moving shadow

4.3.3.1 The Idea

A shadow moves according to its strategy, which can be chosen by the programmer. A strategy decides where to place the shadow by assessing the available location information of its dependent agents. We will discuss some possible strategies in Chapter 4.3.4.

To be able to move a shadow the protocol has to guarantee the reachability of the shadow for both the agents depending on it, and the application, e.g. to terminate agents. The problem is solved as follows: whenever a shadow moves, it leaves a shadow proxy behind. An agent that requests a new time quantum contacts the place from which it received the last time quantum. If the shadow has just moved for the first time, the agent contacts the home place of the shadow. The request is forwarded along the shadow proxy path to the shadow. The shadow answers the request, and transfers its new location. The agent stores this new location to send its next request directly to the shadow. If the application needs to contact the shadow, then this request is sent along the shadow proxy path as well (see Figure 4-13).

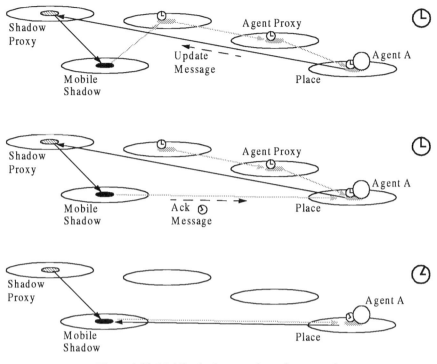

Figure 4-13. Mobile shadows: update of proxy paths

Additionally we associate a time quantum with the shadow. At regular intervals the shadow contacts the home place to update the proxy's information and to get a new *ttl*. Now the shadow proxies containing the old, superfluous path could be removed, if not some agents might still refer to one place along the shadow proxy path. Figure 4-14 illustrates this problem.

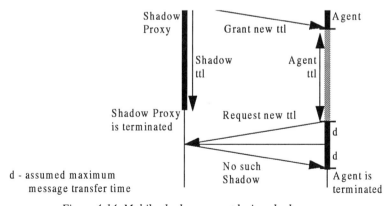

Figure 4-14. Mobile shadows: agent losing shadow proxy

To solve this problem the shadow proxy path is left in place until it can be guaranteed that no agent still refers to a shadow proxy along the path. To do this we have to take into account that the agent might have problems to contact the shadow proxy (see Figure 4-5). This leaves us with a maximum time of $ttl_s + ttl_a + 2(n+1)d$, with d as the assumed maximum message transfer time, ttl_s as the shadow's ttl, and ttl_a as the time quantum allotted to the agent, after which the shadow proxy path can safely be removed. One exception has to be made though; the proxy at the home place can only be removed if the shadow returns.

A few facts can be noted: firstly, if a shadow moves, then after at most $ttl_a + 2(n+1)d$ the information in the agents about the location of their shadow is updated, secondly, by piggy-backing the information on the normal grant message no additional message has to be sent. Furthermore, by duplicating all information of the shadow in its proxies, which can be done when the shadow leaves a place, the protocol can be made more fault-tolerant. If a request cannot be forwarded to the shadow itself, e.g. because a network partition prevents communication, the last reachable proxy shadow can grant a new ttl to the agent. This might lead to problems if the remaining ttl of the path is shorter than the agent ttl, and thus the home place of the shadow is returned as its new location, thus redirecting the agent's next ttl request to the beginning of the new path.

4.3.3.2 The Protocol

We will discuss the extension of the basic protocol to implement mobile shadows (we again omit the functionality limiting the path length); the extension of the hierarchical shadow protocol, while more complex to describe, is analogous. As before, we discuss the different parts separately.

Moving the Shadow. Moving a shadow to another place involves the sending of the shadow from source place to target place and the starting of a timer (signalling that the shadow proxy can be removed). Additionally the shadow's ttl is set to a negative value to disable the regular decrements and the request for a new shadow ttl (action **move()**).

If the shadow comes back to its home place, the shadow proxy is replaced by the original (see action **ReceiveShadow**). When the timer signals then the shadow proxy path is no longer needed, i.e. the shadow has contacted its home shadow proxy and no agent still refers to one of the shadow proxies. Thus the shadow proxy is removed (action **ShadowProxyPathTimeOut**). If the application needs to remove the shadow, it simply calls the shadow's terminateShadow( )-method, which sends a message along the path and removes the local copy of the shadow (i.e. the shadow proxy). Every time the message is received it is forwarded along the path and the local copy removed, until the shadow itself is reached.

move (target)	if (shadowTTL != 0)
	{
	    Send (target, <"MobileShadow", this>);
	    if (currentPlace != null)
	    {
	        // shadow TTL + agent TTL + time-out
	        pathTimeOut = shadowTTL + timeToLive + timeOut;
	        startTimer (pathTimeOut, shadow);
	        shadowTTL = -1;
	    }
	    currentPlace = target;
	}

ReceiveShadow:	[a message <"MobileShadow", shadow> has arrived]
	Receive (<"MobileShadow", shadow>);
	if (shadow.shadowTTL != 0)
	    if (shadow.homePlace != place.name ( ))
	    {
	        shadow.currentPlace = place.name ( );
	        shadowList.add (shadow);
	    }
	    else
	    {
	        // shadow comes back home
	        surrogateId = shadow.shadowId;
	        surrogate = shadowList.find (surrogateId);
	        shadowList.remove (surrogate);
	        shadowList.add (shadow);
	        shadow.currentPlace = null;
	    }

ShadowProxyPath-TimeOut:	[the timer triggered a <timer, shadow> message] Receive (<timer, shadow>); shadowList.remove(shadow);

terminateShadow ( )	if (currentPlace != null)
	    // shadow moved
	    Send (currentPlace, <"Terminate", shadowId>);
	delete (this);

ReceiveTerminate:	[a message <"Terminate", shadowId> has been received]
	shadow = shadowList.find (shadowId);
	if (shadow != null)
	    shadow.terminateShadow ( );

Algorithm 4-19. Mobile shadows: mobility and communication

Algorithm 4-20 contains the additions to the place method called at regular intervals to implement mobile shadows. Every time this method is called all shadows located on a place are checked. If a shadow is not at its home place (i.e. the shadow has moved to this place) then its *ttl* is decremented. If it drops to 0, then a check message is sent home (thereby updating the location information at home), a timer is started and the shadow enters the check phase.

```
Regular Intervals:     for each agent
                       {
                           agent.timeToLive - -;
                           if ( agent.timeToLive == 0 )
                           {
                               shadowId = agent.shadowId;
                               Send (   agent.shadowHome, <"Chk", currentPlace,
                                            shadowId, agent.id> );
                               startTimer ( min ( localTimeOut, agent.timeOut ),
                                            agent.proxy, agent );
                           }
                       }
                       for each shadow
                       {
                           if ( shadow.homePlace != place.name ( ) )
                           {
                               // only if not at home place
                               shadow.timeToLive--;
                               if ( shadow.timeToLive == 0 )
                               {
                                   Send (   shadow.homePlace, <"Chk",
                                                currentPlace, shadow.id> );
                                   startTimer ( "Chk", shadow.timeOut, shadow );
                               }
                           }
                       }
```

Algorithm 4-20. Mobile shadows: extended methods for regular intervals

Shadow Check Phase. The check message is received by the place on which the shadow has been created. If the shadow proxy cannot be found in the list of shadows then it has to have been removed by the application. In this case no message is sent back, subsequently leading to the removal of the shadow and the termination of all dependent agents. If the shadow proxy is found then its information about the location of the shadow is updated and a new *ttl* is sent back. When this new *ttl* is received by the place on which the shadow resides, the timer that has been started when the check message was sent is then stopped, and the shadow's *ttl* is set to the new value. This ends the check phase of the shadow.

ReceiveShadowCheck:	[a message <"Chk", from, shadowId> arrived]
	Receive ("Chk", from, shadowId>);
	shadow = shadowList.find (shadowId);
	if (shadow != null)
	{
	   shadow.currentPlace = place;
	   Send (from,
	         <"Allowance", shadowId, shadow.timeToLive>);
	}

ReceiveShadowAllowance:	[a message <"Allowance", shadowId, timeToLive> arrived]
	Receive (<"Allowance", shadowId, timeToLive>);
	shadow = shadowList.find (shadowId);
	stopTimer (shadow);
	shadow.timeToLive = timeToLive;

Algorithm 4-21. Mobile shadows: checking the shadow

Agent Check Phase. In the basic protocol the agent's check message is simply sent back to the home place of the shadow. With mobile shadows the request is sent to the place from which the last grant has been received. There a timer had been started when this new *ttl* had been sent. This timer is stopped. If the shadow is still on this place, then a new time quantum is handed out. If the shadow has already moved on, the request is forwarded along the path of shadow proxies to the shadow. Then the timer for the time-out signalling that the agent has been terminated is restarted and the grant sent back to the requesting agent (action **ReceiveAgentCheck**). When the new *ttl* is received by the agent, then the associated timer, signalling that the agent has to be terminated, is stopped, the agent's *ttl* and the agent proxy's *ttl* are set to the new value, and the information about the location of the shadow is updated.

ReceiveAgent-
Allowance:
	[a message <"Allowance", shadowPlace, agentId, timeToLive> arrived]
	Receive (<"Allowance", shadowId, agentId, timeToLive>);
	stopTimer (agentId);
	agent = agentList.findAgent (agentId);
	agent.timeToLive = timeToLive;
	agent.proxy.setTTL (timeToLive);
	agent.shadowHome = shadowPlace;

Algorithm 4-22. Mobile shadows: extending the agent's life

```
ReceiveAgentCheck:        [ a message <"Chk", from, shadowId, agentId> arrived ]
                          Receive ( "Chk", from, shadowId, agentId );
                          stopTimer ( agentId );
                          shadow = shadowList.find ( shadowId );
                          if ( shadow.currentPlace != place.name ( ) )
                              Send (   currentPlace,
                                       <"Chk", from, shadowId, agentId> );
                          else
                          {
                              timeToLive = shadow.timeToLive ( from, agentId );
                              if ( timeToLive > 0 )
                              {
                                  startTimer ( shadow.getTimeOut ( agentId )
                                              + timeToLive, shadow, agentId );
                                  Send (   from,
                                           <"Allowance", currentPlace, agentId,
                                            timeToLive> );
                              }
                          }
```

Algorithm 4-22. Mobile shadows: extending the agent's life

Time-outs. In the basic protocol a timer is started when the *ttl* is sent to the agent. If after this time-out no request has been received by the shadow, then the agent has to have been terminated. But if a shadow has moved to another place in the meantime, then only the shadow proxy is notified. Thus if the time-out occurs, then first the agent is removed from the shadow's or shadow proxy's list, and afterwards, if this is only a shadow proxy, then a message signalling that an agent has been removed from the list is sent along the path (action **AgentRequestTimeOut**). If this message is received on a place then the shadow or shadow proxy is identified, the agent is removed from its list, and again sent onward until it reaches the shadow itself (action **ReceiveRemoved**).

```
AgentRequestTimeOut:      [ the timer triggered a <timer, shadow, agentId> message ]
                          Receive ( <timer, shadow, agentId> );
                          shadow.remove ( agentId );
                          if ( shadow.currentPlace != place.name ( ) )
                              Send (   currentPlace,
                                       <"Removed", shadow.shadowId, agentId> );
```

Algorithm 4-23. Mobile shadows: detecting terminated agents

```
ReceiveRemoved:        [ a message <"Removed", shadowId, agentId> has arrived ]
                       Receive ( <"Removed", shadowId, agentId> );
                       shadow = shadowList.find ( shadowId );
                       if ( shadow != null )
                       {
                           shadow.remove ( agentId );
                           if ( shadow.currentPlace != place.name ( ) )
                               Send (   currentPlace,
                                        <"Removed", shadowId, agentId> );
                       }
```

Algorithm 4-23. Mobile shadows: detecting terminated agents

Failures in the Shadow Proxy Path. Two approaches are possible to deal with a broken shadow proxy path. The first approach keeps the exact semantics of the protocol presented so far, but is only able to tolerate short-term failures. The second approach allows for longer failures, but has the drawback of changing the protocol semantics.

The first approach assumes a failure to be only short-term. A shadow proxy along the path that is not able to reach its successor, tries to contact it again until it succeeds. The problem with this approach is that the maximum time that a failure can exist without the protocol itself failing, must exceed the time-out for the agent check phase. This does not include the transfer time of the messages (request messages along the path and the grant message). The advantage is that the information at the shadow is updated correctly, i.e. if the request does not reach the shadow in time, then the agent has been terminated, and the agent entry in the shadow is removed.

The second approach allows for longer lasting failures. If a shadow proxy detects a failure while trying to forward an agent's request for a new *ttl* (i.e. it cannot reach its successor), it sends a new *ttl* back to the agent. The shadow proxy has all the information needed to determine a new agent *ttl*, because it is a former shadow. The *ttl* sent back to the agent is the minimum of the normal agent *ttl* and the remaining shadow proxy *ttl*. The new shadow location sent together with the *ttl* is the home place of the shadow. This way, the next request of this agent is sent to the home place of the shadow. If the agent *ttl* is shorter than the shadow proxy *ttl*, then the next request will be sent along the same path of shadow proxies (which is hopefully connected again). If the shadow proxy *ttl* is shorter than the agent *ttl*, then when the agent sends its next request to the home place, the shadow itself will have contacted its home place and updated the location information, i.e. the agent's request is sent directly to the shadow.

The disadvantage is, that with a failure along the shadow proxy path, the information in the shadow might no longer be correct (even after the agents' *ttl*). Without this variant the shadow knows, by the time the agent's *ttl* has passed, where the agent resides. If the shadow does not receive a request from an agent after its *ttl*, then the system has to have terminated the agent, and it removes the associated entry. But with this variant the conclusion might not be correct, i.e. the shadow disregards an agent, which continues to depend on it (and receives its *ttl* from a shadow proxy). However, this holds only true for as long as the failure remains. As soon as the shadow can be reached again, the next request of the agent will again be forwarded to the shadow, which re-enters the agent into its list. The big advantage is the enhanced availability of the shadow proxy path.

An extension of this variant guarantees that even if the mobile shadow itself is lost, the protocol continues correctly. The prerequisite for this extension is that every agent stores the home place of its shadow. First, if a mobile shadow does not request a new *ttl* in time, then it has to have been removed by the system. Thus the shadow proxy at the home place (which in fact was the first shadow), takes over and replaces the shadow that moved out. Second, if an agent is not able to reach either shadow or shadow proxy, it contacts the home place. This way, if the shadow is lost, then all dependent agents will contact the home place, and thus the newly reinstated shadow there. Hence after the *ttl* of the agents the information at the home shadow is updated, and it can e.g. move out again.

The protocol implementing mobile shadows has first been presented by BAUMANN AND ROTHERMEL (1998C), and has been implemented by HÖFFLINGER (1998).

4.3.4 Strategies for Moving the Shadows

The goals of the mobile shadow protocol is to position shadows in a way that allows either lower communication cost, or higher availability, or a speed up of the recognition of failure of the dependent agents, e.g. because one specific agent necessary for the success of the group of dependants is lost. This implies application-specific or even instantiation-specific knowledge, and thus it will normally be the task of the application programmer to select a strategy. But as a starting point and as a proof of concept we have derived a few simple strategies.

The different strategies are implemented according to the *Strategy pattern* given in GAMMA ET AL. (1994), and can be changed on the fly to extend or to modify the behaviour of a mobile shadow. Furthermore, different strategies can be nested, i.e. if a strategy discerns that it cannot be applied, then a fall back strategy can be used. Thus it is no problem to test out new strategies, as long as they conform to the strategy interface.

4.3.4.1 Possible Strategies

Apart from the minimum cost strategy all of the following strategies have been implemented in the MOLE system by HÖFFLINGER (1998), and can be used by every programmer employing the mobile shadows.

Don't Move. The first and simplest strategy is not to move at all. A shadow using this strategy behaves exactly like a non-mobile shadow. If a strategy discovers that it can no longer compute a new location for the shadow, e.g. if the agent that the strategy follows, terminates, then the strategy chooses its fall back. The *Don't Move* strategy normally is the last fall back strategy.

Minimum Cost. By using a performance model akin to that given in STRASSER AND SCHWEHM (1997) the shadow could be placed in a location that minimizes the communication cost with the agents. But the costs associated with the implementation of such a performance model are high; an up-to-date knowledge of the state of the underlying network (network partitions, delay of messages along different paths, network load etc.) along with knowledge about future interactions and movements of dependent agents is needed to compute accurate information. Furthermore, no implementation providing this functionality for the current MOLE system exists. Nevertheless, the mobile shadow protocol is prepared to use such a performance model if it is provided by the system.

Most Dependants. This strategy lets the shadow move to the place with the highest number of dependent agents. The shadow has this knowledge since the agents inform it about their location when requesting a new time quantum. But this knowledge might be slightly outdated, i.e. the shadow should not react to every changed agent location. Instead it delays any move until it has collected the new locations of several agents. The exact delay can be set by the programmer. The clear advantage of this strategy is that most of the *ttl* requests of agents can be answered locally. Furthermore it can be determined very precisely how many dependent agents are residing on the same place as the agent, and thus the time to move on can be detected with local knowledge. This strategy is well suited in cases in which most, but not all of the agents move in concert.

Random Agent. Here the place of one agent, randomly chosen, is used as the target of the shadow migration. After every move a delay is imposed to allow updating the locations of all dependent agents as a basis for the next migration, i.e. the shadow stays immobile for at least the agent *ttl*. Since this strategy is random, it has no advantage over the other strategies.

Priority-Based. One possible solution to the fault-tolerance problem is to place the shadow where an indispensable agent resides. This is done by instructing the shadow to follow this agent's movements. Obviously, this agent can request a new *ttl* locally, but all other agents depending on this shadow have to send their requests along a longer shadow proxy path. If the agent place crashes, then not only is the agent lost, but the shadow as well, leading to the subsequent termination of all agents dependent of the shadow. The strategy takes an agent id as parameter and follows this agent as long as it exists. If the agent has terminated, then a fall back strategy is used. The strategy has a broader use than only to follow one agent. Let us assume the following scenario: a group of agents contains one agent that processes the data gathered by the other agents in the group. At one point in the processing a second agent takes over and the first terminates. The shadow should follow the first one until it terminates, and then it should trail the second agent. If either is lost due to a crash of its place then the group has to be terminated. This can easily be done by nesting the *Priority-Based* strategy with the two agents' ids as parameters.

Owner Agent. This strategy forces the shadow to follow its owner agent. The owner agent is the agent that created the shadow and as such is normally not depending on this shadow. The main benefit is that the owner agent can quickly terminate the dependent agents. Furthermore if the place on which the owner agent resides crashes, then the shadow is removed as well, and subsequently all dependent agents are terminated. The price that has to be paid though is the higher communication cost if the owner agent does not move with its dependent agents.

4.3.5 Possible Optimizations

Common to all presented variants of the Shadow protocol is that every agent requests and receives a *ttl* of its own. This allows for additional functionality in the shadow, which can on a case-by-case basis decide which agents to keep and which to terminate. But in applications where such a distinction is not necessary, and especially, where the tracking of a single agent in contrast to tracking the group as a whole is not necessary, optimizations are possible. As soon as more than one agent belongs to the same shadow, the following can be done:

- If an agent arrives at a place, where other agents dependent on the same shadow (identified by the shadow's unique id) reside already, then the *ttl* of the agents is set to the maximum of the arriving agent's and the other agents' *ttl*s.
- If an agent requests and receives a new *ttl*, then it is shared with all other agents dependent of the same shadow on the agent's place.

But these optimizations lead to a problem: the proxy path to a single agent can be lost. This happens e.g. if an agent receives additional *ttl* from another agent, and the proxy path, still assuming the original *ttl*, is removed. This can in principle continue as long as the shadow exists, i.e. an agent exists without the shadow knowing of it. The interesting point though is that this doesn't matter for the termination of the whole group of agents. If the termination message is sent to all known proxies, then these proxies forward the termination message along all of the paths they are part of. Ultimately this termination message reaches all of the agents, even those no longer directly known to the shadow. The path segment for an agent exists exactly for the current *ttl* of the agent. So if it got additional time, then at that place the agent proxy holds the path from that place for that remaining time. Every time an agent gets additional time from another agent, there exists a valid path to that other agent. So, by first following the path to the other agent, and then the still valid path to the agent no longer known to the shadow, every agent receives the termination message. Thus the missing information in the shadow does not impair the correctness of the protocol. Only for some of the strategies for mobile shadows the missing information leads to worse results, namely for the *Most Dependants* and the *Random Agent* strategy. Thus application-specific strategies will be even more important for mobile shadows, if the optimizations are used.

It is questionable whether the advantages of the optimizations outweigh the disadvantages. Mandatory for the optimizations to work is that more than one agent depending on the same shadow reside on the same place. In a world-wide mobile agent environment the probability for this might not be high enough to make the optimizations worthwhile. This shows the importance of application-specific strategies using additional knowledge about the agents' migrational patterns.

4.3.6 Comparing the Path Availabilities

In Appendix C we discuss the availabilities, both for existence of the path and for locating an agent by following the path, of the path concept and the different variants of the shadow concept in detail. The most important point is, that the basic protocol and the mobile shadow variant have a limiting availability higher than 0, in fact mainly depending on the respective *ttl* used. The hierarchical shadow variant has instead a limiting availability of 0, i.e. the same as the path concept. Thus the most interesting comparison is between these two groups. We choose the path concept and the basic protocol.

Let us summarize the findings for the path availability of the path concept and of the basic protocol.

We use $A_v(t)$ to denote the availability of a node v, and $A_p(t)$ for the availability of the path itself.

The availability for the path concept is (see Equation C-3):

$$A_p(t) = e^{-n\lambda_v t} \qquad \text{(Equation 4-1)}$$

It is clear that the limiting availability, being the limit of $A_p(t)$ as t approaches infinity, is 0:

$$\alpha_p = \lim_{t \to \infty} A_p(t) = \lim_{t \to \infty} e^{-n\lambda_v t} = 0 \qquad \text{(Equation 4-2)}$$

The availability for the basic protocol of the shadow concept is (see Equation C-14):

$$A_p(t) = \frac{1}{n+1} \sum_{k=0}^{n} \left(\frac{\frac{2}{ttl}}{\lambda_v + \frac{2}{ttl}} + \frac{\lambda_v}{\lambda_v + \frac{2}{ttl}} e^{-\left(\lambda_v + \frac{2}{ttl}\right)t} \right)^k \qquad \text{(Equation 4-3)}$$

It can be seen that the limiting availability is a constant value larger than 0. We yield (see Equation C-15):

$$\alpha_p = \frac{1}{n+1}\sum_{k=0}^{n}\alpha_{pk} = \frac{1}{n+1}\sum_{k=0}^{n}\frac{1}{1+k\lambda_v\frac{ttl}{2}} \qquad \text{(Equation 4-4)}$$

Direct comparisons, however, are only possible if we make assumptions about the different failure rates for the nodes and the communication channels, and for the repair rate for the communication channels.

Since these rates vary with the used technology, no generic measurements exist. We choose different sources for these and try to average the values. The sources are: IMEX (1999), a report about high availability computing, STURM (1999), a paper about the management of quality of service, values for the faculty of Computer Science of the University of Stuttgart supplied by FABIAN (1999), for the University of Stuttgart in general provided by BANNAS (1999), and values for a provider network (see USWEST (1999)). All of these following numbers have to be taken with a grain of salt. It has to be emphasized that, while they are as accurate as possible, they are no generic values usable for every possible environment. We use the following values for the MTTF and MTTR of nodes and communication channels. For communication channels the repair functionality is included in our discussion, since they do not hold state that is important for the protocols.

Component	MTTF [hours]	λ [1/hours]	MTTR [hours]	μ [1/hours]	availability
NT machine	87.6	$1.142 \cdot 10^{-2}$	1.2	0.833	$\alpha=0.986$
Unix machine	730	$1.370 \cdot 10^{-3}$	3.3	0.303	$\alpha=0.995$
Communication channel LAN	973	$1.028 \cdot 10^{-3}$	0.5	2.000	$\alpha=0.9995$
Communication channel Backbone	1460	$6.849 \cdot 10^{-4}$	3.0	0.333	$\alpha=0.9998$

Table 4-1. Failure and repair rates for components (in hours)

We define 2 scenarios: in the first, named scenario 1, Unix machines are connected via a backbone communication channel, i.e. we have a high availability of nodes and communication channels, in the second, named scenario 2, NT machines are connected via a LAN, i.e. we have comparatively low availability.

The normal migration time in Java-based systems is around 100-150 ms, and with optimizations could probably be sped up by a factor of 2. Thus we assume a migration time of 50ms, leading us to 20 migrations per second. Since the shortest *ttl* we choose for our scenarios is 1 second, we will take this as the path length for our comparisons.

The Importance of the TTL. Let us first examine the effect of the *ttl* on the availability of the path in the shadow concept. We choose values for the *ttl* between 1 sec and 1 hour, and a length for the path of 20. The results are shown in Figure 4-15. Please note that even a *ttl* of 6 minutes is an extremely high value. The significance of the value for the *ttl* compared to the different availabilities of the path components is clearly shown, since the graphs for different availabilities with constant *ttl* cannot be distinguished without magnification (see Figure 4-15(a)). Only enlarged as in Figure 4-15(b) can the difference be identified.

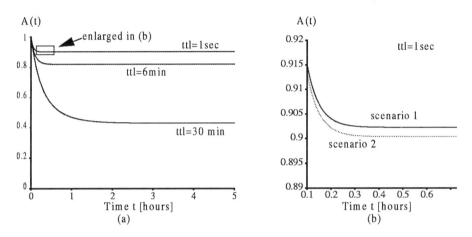

Figure 4-15. Shadow concept: path availability depending on failure rate and ttl (high availability=black, low availability=grey, n=20)

Shadow Concept vs. Path Concept. Let us now compare the basic protocol against the path concept. We choose the two scenarios and a comparatively high value for the *ttl* of 6 minutes. We see in Figure 4-16 that the shadow concept is nearly unaffected by the changing availability. The availability of the path concept, however, is clearly affected. This shows also in the graphs for the difference of the availabilities. There it becomes clear, that for worse availabilities of nodes and communication channels, the shadow concept performs even better in comparison to the path concept.

A second point can be concluded from Figure 4-16: if an agent exists for only a short period, then the path concept and the shadow concept are nearly equal in availability. In fact, the availability for shadow concept and path concept are exactly the same, until the first check phase is initiated (this has not been modelled in the computations of the availabilities. Thus for short durations the path concept, having a lower overhead, is the better choice.

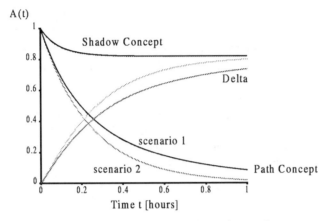

Figure 4-16. Shadow concept: basic protocol vs. path concept (n=20)

4.3.7 Discussion

The Shadow protocol in its different variants supports asynchronous operation, albeit with the constraint, that every agent has to contact its shadow at regular intervals. The two messages needed for receiving a new *ttl* are the only cost in the basic protocol. No cost is introduced by either establishing the agent proxy paths or removing it. As we have seen in the comparison of basic protocol and path concept, the availability is higher. The only exception are very short-lived agents, for which the path concept provides the same availability.

For the hierarchical shadows, the availability is lower, since the path connecting the hierarchical shadows is not repaired, i.e. we have the same problem as with the path concept, albeit on average with a much shorter path.

The mobile shadows provide an availability slightly worse than the basic protocol, but they provide additional functionality; the programmer is now able to modify the shadow location depending on the locations of the depending agents.

5 Distributed Garbage Collection

Algorithms for garbage collection are important for the memory management of programming languages supporting dynamic objects. BLOOM AND ZDONICK (1987) observed that programmer-controlled memory management is notoriously error-prone. The most prominent example is the C++ language. According to BOEHM (1998), 30 to 40% of development time is devoted to storage management for programs that manipulate complex linked data structures. The problem gets even more complex if garbage collection is to be used in distributed systems. SHAPIRO ET AL. (1994) describe the problems in detail. Some examples of distributed garbage collectors are:

- Stub-Scion-Pair chains, desribed in SHAPIRO, DICKMAN AND PLAINFOSSÉ (1992A), as a general garbage collection mechanism for distributed systems.
- the garbage collector for the distributed database Thor. Detailed information to this garbage collector can be found in MAHESHWARI AND LISKOV (1997).
- the garbage collector of Argus, an implementation of a reference counting scheme. LISKOV (1988) describes Argus, and programming using Argus, and DETLEFS (1990) discusses the shortcomings of this garbage collector in concurrent systems.
- the garbage collector of Emerald, a modified mark-and-sweep implementation. An introduction to Emerald can be found in JUL ET AL. (1988).

In addition, some modern distributed programming environments allow dynamic object migration, which further complicates storage management. Examples are the system Orca described in BAL AND TANENBAUM (1990), where dynamic object migration is used as part of the run time environment, the system Arjuna as described in CAUGHEY AND SHRIVASTAVA (1995), and the communication support provided by LEVY AND TEMPERO (1991).

After the description of the system and failure model used throughout this chapter follows a short introduction into distributed garbage collection and a presentation of the distributed garbage collection algorithms of importance to the transformations presented in Chapter 6.

5.1 System and Failure Models

We assume the following system model for this chapter: a finite set of concurrently executing processes is considered that communicate by passing messages through channels with infinite buffers. We assume no particular message ordering for the communication channels. When an algorithm makes an additional assumption we will point it out explicitly.

The failure model assumes neither process nor channel failures, i.e. no failures at all. This is the failure model used by most publications describing garbage collection *algorithms*. Even recent publications handling active objects and object migration, e.g. KAFURA, MUKHERJI AND WASHABAUGH (1995) or PIQUER (1996) employ this failure model.

Publications describing distributed garbage collection *implementations* (see e.g. CAUGHEY AND SHRIVASTAVA (1995)) tend to use the system and failure model presented in Chapter 3.

5.2 Introduction to Distributed Garbage Collection

The basic functionality of distributed garbage collection is to reclaim storage of inaccessible objects distributed over multiple nodes. This is done by considering a program's data as a graph, whose edges represent references to objects and whose vertices represent the objects themselves. A distinguished set of vertices is named the set of root objects. These objects are never garbage-collected. Objects reachable from this set of root objects are called alive; all others are unreachable and are considered to be garbage. Two different classes of algorithms have been developed for distributed garbage collection, namely reference counting algorithms and mark-and-sweep algorithms. An overview of algorithms can be found in PLAINFOSSÉ AND SHAPIRO (1995). ABDULLAHI AND RINGWOOD (1998) present a survey, in which they evaluate these algorithms. Reference counting algorithms maintain a counter with the number of references to each object. As soon as this counter drops to zero, the system can conclude that the object is garbage, and can consequently remove the object. The disadvantage is that reference counting can be incomplete in the sense that only acyclic graphs are collected correctly. Objects involved in cyclic references (e.g. referencing one another) cannot be collected. Mark-and-sweep algorithms walk through the graph, beginning with the root set, to determine the living objects. Mark-and-sweep algorithms are complete (i.e. all garbage is identified and subsequently removed), but they need global synchronization phases and more cooperation from the objects in the graph than reference counting algorithms. In Chapter 6, we will transform some of the algorithms into control algorithms for mobile agents. We only consider the class of reference counting algorithms, because the cost for mark-and-sweep algorithms combined with the global synchronization phases make them unsuitable for the use in mobile agent systems. Furthermore, as RUDALICS (1990A) states, in a distributed environment reference counting seems to have two advantages over mark-and-sweep algorithms: firstly, only nodes holding references are involved in its reclamation, i.e. not all nodes of the distributed system participate in the reclamation of one object. Secondly, communication patterns of reference counting systems in general match the communication patterns of the underlying application.

5.2.1 A Computation Model for Distributed Objects

We now introduce the computation model used in the presentation of the different garbage collection schemes. An object-oriented distributed system consists of a collection of objects communicating with each other via messages. A subset of this collection is a set of *root objects*, that will never be collected by the garbage collector. Objects are able to hold *references* to other objects. We will call a reference to an object r an r-reference. If an object s holds an r-reference, then object r is called a *descendant* of s. An object is *reachable* or *alive* if it is either a root object or a descendant of a reachable object. A reachable object s holding an r-reference can *copy* this reference to another object t. To do this, s sends a message to t containing the r-reference. After receiving this message t holds an r-reference, too. An object can have multiple references to the same target. An object s holding an r-reference can *delete* the reference, after which it no longer holds this r-reference. If this was the last reference from s to r, then s is no longer able to reach r (unless it receives a new reference to r).

CR_s:	[s is reachable and holds an r-reference] Send (t, <copy r>);
RC_t:	[a message <copy r> arrived] Receive (<copy r>); insert r-reference;
DR_s:	[s holds an r-reference] delete r-reference;

Algorithm 5-1. Reference manipulation by objects

Each of the actions is assumed to be executed atomically. An action subscripted with s takes place in object s. An assertion between brackets is a guard, guaranteeing that the action can only be executed if the assertion is true. An object s can initiate the copying of an r-reference (action CR_s), it can insert an r-reference (action RC_t) that has been received as a result of the action CR_s, and it can delete an r-reference (action DR_s). Since we only consider non-cyclic references, our definition of the term garbage is slightly relaxed compared to that of normal garbage collection. An object is called *garbage* if there are no references to it. A garbage collector will eventually find all objects that are garbage and collect them.

5.3 Reference Counting Schemes

Reference counting schemes can be divided into 2 groups:
- Direct Reference Counting Algorithms.
- Indirect Reference Counting Algorithms.

The first group contains simple reference counting, the Lermen and Maurer variant, and the Rudalics variants, the second group weighted reference counting and local reference counting. We will now examine these different schemes in more detail.

5.3.1 Direct Reference Counting Algorithms

All algorithms in this class directly count the number of references in the system. As soon as the number of r-references is 0, the object r is garbage and can be collected. Every time an r-reference is copied, an *increment* message is sent to the object r. A *copy* message (containing the r-reference) is sent to the receiving node. An *ack* message is sent by one of the participants, depending on the algorithm. It has to be guaranteed by the algorithm that this *ack* message is correctly received before a *decrement* message is sent by one of the participants. Since all of the discussed mechanisms use the same mechanism to signal the deletion of an r-reference, namely a simple *decrement* message without *ack* message, we concentrate in the graphical representation on the copying of references. Three nodes participate, depicted as squares. We assume that node R contains object r, node S contains object s with an r-reference that copies this reference to object t on node T.

5.3.1.1 Simple Reference Counting

The simplest solution to reference counting is to send *increment* messages to the object before a reference is copied. The *increment* message is acknowledged by sending the *ack* message, and only after the reception of the *ack* message the *copy* message is sent. A *decrement* message can only be sent by s after the *inc* message has been acknowledged.

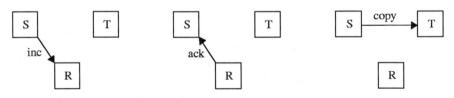

Figure 5-1. Simple reference counting

The protocol for simple reference counting is given in Algorithm 5-2.

$Init_r$:	**integer** $r.refCount_r = 0$;
CR_s:	[$s.refCount_s > 0$ or s is root object, and holds an r-reference] Send (r, <increment r, s, t>);
RI_r:	[a message <increment r, s, t> arrived] Receive (<increment r, s, t>); $r.refCount_r = r.refCount_r + 1$; Send (s, <ack r, t>);
RA_s:	[a message <ack r, t> arrived] Receive (<ack r, t>); Send (t, <copy r>);
RC_t:	[a message <copy r> arrived] Receive (<copy r>); insert the r-reference;
DR_t:	[t holds an r-reference] Send (r, <decrement r>); delete r-reference;
RD_r:	[a message <decrement r> arrived] Receive (<decrement r>); $r.refCount_r = r.refCount_r - 1$; **if** ($r.refCount_r == 0$) delete r;

Algorithm 5-2. Simple reference counting

5.3.1.2 The Variant of Lermen and Maurer

The variant of Lermen and Maurer has been designed to overcome the need to wait for the *ack* messages before sending the *copy* message (this variant has been presented in LERMEN AND MAURER (1986)). The main difference to the simple reference counting algorithm is that the *ack* message is sent to the target node T instead of the source node S. While in the simple reference counting scheme the reference on the source node can only be deleted after receipt of the *ack* message, here it is the target node that has to wait for the *ack* message. Thus the *increment* and the *copy* message can be sent within one action, without having to wait for the *ack* message. An additional assumption is made about the communication channel in this variant.

Figure 5-2. The Lermen & Maurer variant

The channels are assumed to have the FIFO property. Otherwise, a *decrement* message sent by S after the *increment* message could arrive earlier at R than the *increment* message possibly leading to an incorrect collection of r. The protocol for the Lermen and Maurer variant is given in Algorithm 5-3.

$Init_r$:	**integer** $r.\text{refCount}_r = 0$;
CR_s:	[s is reachable and holds an r-reference] Send (r, <increment r, t>); Send (t, <copy r>);
RI_r:	[a message <increment r, t> arrived] Receive (<increment r, t>); $r.\text{refCount}_r = r.\text{refCount}_r + 1$; Send (t, <ack r>);
RC_t:	[a message <copy r> arrived] Receive (<copy r>); insert the r-reference; if ($t.\text{unAckdRefs}_r < 0$) $t.\text{ackdRefs}_r = t.\text{ackdRefs}_r + 1$; $t.\text{unAckdRefs}_r = t.\text{unAckdRefs}_r + 1$;
RA_t:	[a message <ack r> arrived] Receive (<ack r>); if ($t.\text{unAckdRefs}_r > 0$) $t.\text{ackdRefs}_r = t.\text{ackdRefs}_r + 1$; $t.\text{unAckdRefs}_r = t.\text{unAckdRefs}_r - 1$;
DR_t:	[t holds an r-reference and $t.\text{ackdRefs}_r > 0$] $t.\text{ackdRefs}_r = t.\text{ackdRefs}_r - 1$; Send (r, <decrement r>); delete r-reference;
RD_r:	[a message <decrement r> arrived] Receive (<decrement r>); $r.\text{refCount}_r = r.\text{refCount}_r - 1$; if ($r.\text{refCount}_r == 0$) delete r;

Algorithm 5-3. The Lermen & Maurer variant

The correct deletion of references is more complicated in the Lermen and Maurer variant than in the simple reference counting algorithm. A safe (i.e. correct) assumption is that a reference in an object can be deleted as long as the number of *copy* and *ack* messages is equal and larger 0. This condition ensures that there are still references that can be deleted and that all of them have been acknowledged. But this condition can be slightly relaxed. It is enough to ensure that both are larger 0. While not ensuring that all references have been acknowledged, it guarantees that at least one of them has been acknowledged. To implement this relaxed condition we define two counters ackdRefs_r and unAckdRefs_r containing the number of acknowledged and unacknowledged references, respectively. Every time a <copy *r*>-message is received, unAckdRefs$_r$ has to be incremented. Every time an <ack *r*>-message is received, ackdRefs$_r$ is incremented and unAckdRefs$_r$ decremented. But it can happen that *ack* messages arrive before the corresponding *copy* messages. An additional counter could be introduced to manage these early *ack* messages. An alternative is to use negative values in unAckdRefs$_r$ to encode this information. Thus, if an <ack *r*>-message is received, ackdRefs$_r$ is only incremented if unAckdRefs$_r$ has a positive value, and unAckdRefs$_r$ is decremented (action **RA$_t$**). Accordingly, if a <copy *r*>-message is received, ackdRefs$_r$ is incremented together with unAckdRefs$_r$, if that value is negative (action **RC$_t$**). If an object wants to delete an *r*-reference it has to be ensured that ackdRefs$_r$ is larger than 0. If this condition holds, ackdRefs$_r$ is decremented, a <decrement *r*>-message is sent to the object *r*, and the *r*-reference is deleted (action **DR$_r$**).

5.3.1.3 The 3 Message Variant of Rudalics

Two variants of the Lermen & Maurer scheme have been proposed by RUDALICS (1988). In the 3 message variant of Rudalics the *increment* message is still sent from node S to R, but the *copy* message now is sent by node R. The third message, the *ack* message, is sent from T to S.

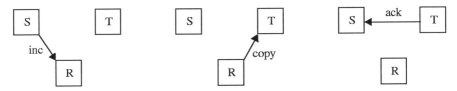

Figure 5-3. The Rudalics variant with 3 messages

The protocol for the Rudalics variant with 3 messages is given in Algorithm 5-4.

Init$_r$:	integer *r*.refCount$_r$ = 0;
CR$_s$:	[*s* is reachable and holds an *r*-reference] *s*.unAckd$_r$ = *s*.unAckd$_r$ + 1; Send (*r*, <increment *r*, *s*, *t*>);
RI$_r$:	[a message <increment *r*, *s*, *t*> arrived] Receive (<increment *r*, *s*, *t*>); *r*.refCount$_r$ = *r*.refCount$_r$ + 1; Send (*t*, <copy *r*, *s*>);
RC$_t$:	[a message <copy *r*, *s*> arrived] Receive (<copy *r*, *s*>); insert the *r*-reference; Send(*s*, <ack *r*>);

Algorithm 5-4. The Rudalics variant with 3 messages

RA$_s$:	[a message <ack r> arrived] Receive (<ack r>); $s.\text{unAckd}_r = s.\text{unAckd}_r - 1$;
DR$_t$:	[t holds an r-reference and $t.\text{unAckd}_r == 0$] Send (r, <decrement r>); delete r-reference;
RD$_r$:	[a message <decrement r> arrived] Receive (<decrement r>); $r.\text{refCount}_r = r.\text{refCount}_r - 1$; if ($r.\text{refCount}_r == 0$) delete r;

Algorithm 5-4. The Rudalics variant with 3 messages

In this variant a counter of unacknowledged copies unAckd$_r$ is used. If an object wants to delete an r-reference (action **DR$_t$**), then the precondition that unAckd$_r$ is 0 ensures that for every copy operation an <ack r>-message has been received. This is important because in this variant no FIFO-channel is assumed for the communication. A <decrement r>-message is sent to r and the r-reference is deleted. On receipt of a <decrement r>-message the object r decrements its reference counter, and as soon as the reference count is 0 deletes itself (action **RD$_r$**).

5.3.1.4 The 4 Message Variant of Rudalics

The 4 message variant (presented in RUDALICS (1988)) additionally sends a *copy* message from node S to node T together with the *increment* message sent to R. The *ack* message is sent from T to S after receiving both *copy* messages. Object *s* may only be deleted if all *ack* messages have been received. Interestingly, the *ack* message can also be sent by *t* as soon as two *copy* messages from the same source have been received by *t*. Why? Let us assume that two *copy* messages sent by *s* have been received. This implies that another two *copy* messages will be sent by *r* (leading to the second *ack* message). If one *ack* message is sent back to the object *s*, then *s* still has to wait for the second *ack* message. Thus it is safe to send this first *ack* message.

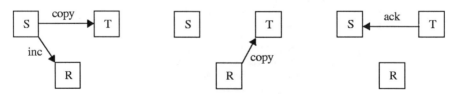

Figure 5-4. The Rudalics variant with 4 messages

The protocol for the Rudalics variant with 4 messages is given in Algorithm 5-5. To implement this variant a *set* has to be employed. A set contains a number of objects. Objects can be added via the method *add* (object), and removed via the method *re-*

move (object). Both return true if the operation was successful. This is used to implement a binary counter for the source (i.e. the object *s*) of a copy message. The variable unAckd$_r$ is used as before in the 3 message variant.

Init$_r$:	**integer** *r*.refCount$_r$ = 0;
CR$_s$:	[*s* is reachable and holds an *r*-reference] *s*.unAckd$_r$ = *s*.unAckd$_r$ + 1; Send (*r*, <increment *r*, *s*, *t*>); Send (*t*, <copy *r*, *s*>);
RI$_r$:	[a message <increment *r*, *s*, *t*> arrived] Receive (<increment *r*, *s*, *t*>); *r*.refCount$_r$ = *r*.refCount$_r$ + 1; Send (*t*, <copy *r*, *s*>);

RC$_t$:	[a message <copy *r*, *s*> arrived]
	Receive (<copy *r*, *s*>);
	if (*t*.rcvdSet$_r$ .remove (*s*) == true)
	    Send(*s*, <ack *r*>);
	else
	{
	    insert *r*-reference;
	    t.rcvdSet$_r$ .add (*s*);
	}

RA$_s$:	[a message <ack *r*> arrived] Receive (<ack *r*>); *s*.unAckd$_r$ = *s*.unAckd$_r$ - 1;
DR$_t$:	[*t* holds an *r*-reference and *t*.unAckd$_r$ == 0] Send (*r*, <decrement *r*>); delete *r*-reference;

RD$_r$:	[a message <decrement *r*> arrived]
	Receive (<decrement *r*>);
	r.refCount$_r$ = *r*.refCount$_r$ - 1;
	if (*r*.refCount$_r$ == 0)
	    delete *r*;

Algorithm 5-5. The Rudalics variant with 4 messages

5.3.2 Weighted Reference Counting

Weighted reference counting associates with every reference a weight. WRC schemes have first been proposed by BEVAN (1989) and by WATSON AND WATSON (1987). If a reference is copied, the associated weight is divided between original and copy. No interaction is necessary with the object *r* itself for copying a reference; the need for synchronization with *r* can be avoided. If a reference is deleted, a *decrement* message with the weight associated to this reference is sent to the object. The object stores the weight it has given out, and as soon as the sum of weights sent back is the same as the sum of weights handed out it is guaranteed that no references exist any longer. Sooner or later the weight associated to a reference is no longer divisible, i.e. the reference can no longer be copied. In this case, new weight can be requested from the object to remedy this situation.

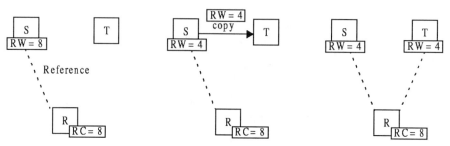

Figure 5-5. Weighted reference counting
(RC = reference count, RW = reference weight).

The protocol for the weighted reference counting variant is given in Algorithm 5-6. The version of the protocol presented here guarantees the following: if an *r*-reference is to be copied and its weight is no longer divisible, then this *r*-reference will not be deleted until additional weight has been granted and the *copy* message sent. Furthermore, we assume that a weight is divisible by 2 without remainder. This can be assured by choosing new weight suitably. Each object *r* initializes on creation a variable refWeight$_r$, which contains the weight given out by this object (action **Init$_r$**). If an object *s* wants to send a copy of an *r*-reference to *t* (action **CR$_s$**), the associated weight$_r$ is split between the *r*-reference held by *s* and the copy that is sent to *t*. If weight$_r$ is no longer divisible, a request to grant more weight is sent to *r*. If a <copy *r*, weight>-message is received (action **RC$_t$**), then, if an *r*-reference already exists, the received weight is added to weight$_r$. If no *r*-reference exists, it is inserted and weight$_r$ is set to the received weight. If object *r* receives a request for more weight (action **RR$_r$**), it sends new weight back to the requesting object and adds the new weight granted to its reference weight refWeight$_r$. If a <GrantWeight *r*, newweight *t*>-message is received, then the new weight is added to the (indivisible) weight, and the delayed *copy* message sent to *t* (action **RW$_s$**).

Init$_r$:	**integer** $r.\text{refWeight}_r = 0$;

CR$_s$:	[s is reachable, holds an r-reference and $\text{w\_req}_r = \text{false}$]
	if ($s.\text{weight}_r$ DIV $2 > 0$)
	{
	    Send (t, <copy r, $s.\text{weight}_r$ DIV 2>);
	    $s.\text{weight}_r = s.\text{weight}_r$ DIV 2;
	}
	else
	{
	    Send (r, <RequestWeight, s, t>);
	    $\text{w\_req}_r = \text{true}$;
	}

RC$_t$:	[a message <copy r, weight> arrived]
	Receive (<copy r, weight>);
	if (defined r-reference)
	    $t.\text{weight}_r = t.\text{weight}_r + \text{weight}$;
	else
	{
	    insert the r-reference;
	    $t.\text{weight}_r = \text{weight}$;
	}

RR$_r$:	[a message <Request Weight, s, t> arrived] Receive (<Request Weight, s, t>); Send (s, <GrantWeight r, newWeight, t>); $r.\text{refWeight}_r = r.\text{refWeight}_r + \text{newWeight}$;
RW$_s$:	[a message <GrantWeight r, newWeight, t> arrived] Receive (<Weight r, newWeight, t>); $s.\text{weight}_r = s.\text{weight}_r + \text{newWeight}$; Send (t, <copy r, $s.\text{weight}_r$ DIV 2>); $s.\text{weight}_r = s.\text{weight}_r$ DIV 2; $\text{w\_req}_r = \text{false}$;
DR$_t$:	[t holds an r-reference with $t.\text{weight}_r$ and $\text{w\_req}_r = \text{false}$] Send (r, <decrement r, $t.\text{weight}_r$>); delete r-reference;
RD$_r$:	[a message <decrement r, weight> arrived] Receive (<decrement r, weight>); $r.\text{refWeight}_r = r.\text{refWeight}_r - \text{weight}$; if ($r.\text{refWeight}_r == 0$) delete r;

Algorithm 5-6. Weighted reference counting

When an object t deletes an r-reference, it sends a <decrement r, weight$_r$>-message to the object r, returning the weight of the deleted r-reference (action **DR$_t$**). Upon receipt of a <decrement r, weight$_r$>-message object r subtracts the received weight from the reference count refCount$_r$. Object r can be deleted if its reference count drops to 0 (action **RD$_t$**).

5.3.3 Local Reference Counting

Local reference counting differentiates between local and remote counting of references on a node (the idea has been proposed independently by ICHISUGI AND YONEZAWA (1990), RUDALICS (1990A) and PIQUER (1991)). For this scheme on every node on which references to an object exist, a local counter is instantiated. If a copy of a reference is made on a node, then the local counter is incremented. If a reference is sent to another node, two different situations may arise. If no reference to that object exists on the target node, a new counter is instantiated (set to 1), and the node identifier of the source node is stored with it. If a reference to that object exists already, then the counter on the target node is incremented (to reflect the new local reference), and a *decrement* message is sent back to the sending node. This rule guarantees that the graph of references forms a simple tree. If a reference to an object is discarded, then the local counter is decremented. If the number of local references is decremented to 0, then a *decrement* message is sent to the node whose identifier was stored with the local reference counter.

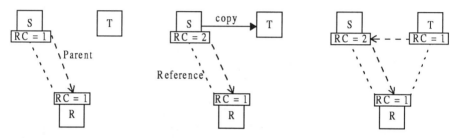

Figure 5-6. Local reference counting

This variant is especially suited to support mobile objects, because the migration of an object from one node to another can be modelled very naturally. This is done by installing a new counter for the migrating object containing all the reference counts of the object, and the target node of the object as the node identifier. An example for an implementation of local reference counting are the Stub Scion Pair (SSP) chains (SHAPIRO, DICKMAN AND PLAINFOSSÉ (1992B)).

The protocol for the local reference counting variant is given in Algorithm 5-7. On creation each object r initializes a variable lrc_r in which it counts the number of references to itself, and a variable $parent_r$ set to null (action **Init$_r$**). Furthermore, for every newly received x-reference a counter lrc_x is instantiated. This variable is used to count the number of local x-references. If an object s wants to copy an r-reference, it sends an $<s, copy\ r>$-message to the receiving object t and increments its local reference counter lrc_r (action **CR$_s$**). If an $<s, copy\ r>$-message is received by object t (action **RC$_t$**), first the r-reference is inserted. Now the local reference count lrc_r is inspected. If it is 0, then this is the first r-reference received by object t. The local reference count lrc_r is set to 1 to reflect the number of local references and the variable $parent_r$ (i.e. the object from which the first r-reference has been received) is set to object s. If lrc_r is already larger than 0, then another r-reference and thus a parent object (specified in variable $parent_r$) already exists. In this case, lrc_r is incremented by one to reflect the new copy of the r-reference and a <decrement r>-message is sent back to object s. When an object t deletes an r-reference (action $\mathbf{DR_t}$), it decrements the local reference counter lrc_r. If lrc_r is 0, then the following conditions hold: 1. no r-reference remains in the object t, and 2. no object q holds an r-reference for which $parent_r$ (in object q) equals object t. Now either object t has initially received an r-reference from another object, in which case $parent_r$ is not null. A <decrement r>-message is sent to this object. The other possible case is that the object t has not received an r-reference before holding one. This is the case if $parent_r$ is null. The object t has to be the object r itself and can thus be deleted. Upon receipt of a <decrement r>-message lrc_r is decremented (action $\mathbf{RD_s}$). If lrc_r drops to 0, then the same happens as in action $\mathbf{DR_t}$.

$\mathbf{Init_r}$:	**integer** $r.lrc_r = 0$; **Object** $r.parent_r$ = null;
$\mathbf{CR_s}$:	[s is reachable and holds an r-reference] Send (t, <s, copy r>); $s.lrc_r = s.lrc_r + 1$;

$\mathbf{RC_t}$:	[a message <s, copy r> arrived]
	Receive (<s, copy r>);
	insert the r-reference;
	if($t.lrc_r == 0$)
	{
	    $t.lrc_r = 1$;
	    $t.parent_r = s$;
	}
	else
	{
	    Send (s, <decrement r>);
	    $t.lrc_r = t.lrc_r + 1$;
	}

$\mathbf{DR_t}$:	[t holds an r-reference]
	$t.lrc_r = t.lrc_r - 1$;
	delete r-reference;
	if ($t.lrc_r == 0$)
	{
	    if ($t.parent_r$ == null)
	        delete r;
	    else
	        Send ($t.parent_r$, <decrement r>);
	}

Algorithm 5-7. Local reference counting

```
RD_s:    [ a message <decrement r> arrived ]
         Receive ( <decrement r> );
         s.lrc_r = s.lrc_r - 1;
         if ( s.lrc_r == 0 )
         {
             if ( s.parent_r == null )
                 delete r;
             else
                 Send ( s.parent_r, <decrement r> );
         }
```

Algorithm 5-7. Local reference counting

In an actual implementation the local reference counters would not be instantiated for every object. Instead, *local group reference counters* are used to count all references on a node, so that to the garbage collection mechanism each node looks like one object.

> *"How can I get there?" asked Dorothy.*
> *"You must walk. It is a long journey, through a country that is sometimes pleasant and sometimes dark and terrible."*
>
> L. Frank Baum, The Wizard of Oz

6 From Garbage Collection to Control Mechanisms for Mobile Agents

We have seen in the last chapter that in the area of distributed garbage collection algorithms exist, that detect whether one object is garbage depending on the number of references held by others. These other objects fit our definition of a dependency object in Definition 2-1 quite precisely, if we define a parent relation as "holds reference". The problem of garbage collection is thus similar to the orphan detection problem for mobile agents. Moreover, the path created by local reference counters is similar to the paths in the path concept, i.e. in some algorithms we have an analogue to the problem how an agent can be found. Thus solutions that are similar to those proposed in Chapter 4 for the control of mobile agents have been developed in the area of distributed garbage collection.

TEL AND MATTERN (1993) proved that the class of termination detection algorithms and the class of garbage collection algorithms are identical. Since the design of an algorithm for distributed systems is a non-trivial problem, to have transformations from one problem class to another has the following advantages:

- The possible discovery of algorithms that have already been found in another problem context.
- Simple transfer of the algorithms that have been proven to be correct in another class of the same family, e.g. in TEL AND MATTERN (1993) three new termination detection algorithms have been discovered.

A similar transformation providing the conversion of either of these classes into control algorithms for mobile agents should allow the access to a large number of algorithms for controlling mobile agents. But the failure model of the area of distributed algorithms and of the area of mobile agents are radically different, ruling out the direct use of these mechanisms. Instead we will transform garbage collection algorithms to show the following: all the principles of the transformed algorithms can be found in existing control mechanisms for mobile agents. Thus we will use for this chapter the same system and fault model as in the last chapter.

We model the migration of an agent as copying of the associated objects including references from source to target node, and subsequent deletion of the copies on the source node. Then we introduce dependency objects in one of the following ways:

- Agents are defined as objects referencing a dependency object called γ, i.e. an agent is, regarding the garbage collection mechanism, viewed as the parent object of the dependency object. We define an agent to be an orphan when it holds no dependency object reference. A reference has to be deleted whenever it is detected that the associated object has been removed.

- A dependency object γ is defined as parent object referencing the agents. When an agent is referenced by no dependency object, i.e. if no dependency object holds a reference to this agent, then the algorithm recognizes the agent as garbage / orphan.

Finally, we examine the migration of an agent and its consequences for the participants, i.e. whether the transformation provides orphan detection functionality or functionality to locate an agent. When a transformation provides functionality to locate an agent, we assume the functionality for terminating the agent as well. This generic approach covers all possible dependencies between agents and other objects inside the agent system that are based on a direct relationship, since the definition of a dependency object in Definition 2-1 explicitly allows it to be an agent, an object or even a place inside the agent system.

We start this chapter by presenting the computation model used for the transformations. Then we discuss the different transformations yielded by following the two different approaches. After assessing them we will examine combinations of the most promising transformations. A comparison between these protocols and the protocols that have been developed in Chapter 4 will be presented in Chapter 7.

6.1 A Computation Model for Mobile Agents

The following computation model is in part derived from the basic computation model developed for termination detection in distributed systems (see TEL (1994) for details). This computation model will simplify transforming the garbage control algorithms into control protocols for mobile agents.

The possible actions of an agent are listed in Algorithm 6-1. Each of the actions is assumed to be executed atomically. An action subscripted with A takes place in the agent A. An assertion between brackets is a guard, guaranteeing that the action can only be executed if the assertion is true.

LP_A:	[state == alive] exitPlace();
AP_B:	[state == alive] enterPlace();
SM_A:	[state == alive] Send (<MSG>);
RM_A:	[state == alive, **message** <MSG> arrived] Receive (<MSG>);

Algorithm 6-1. The basic computations of an agent

Agent migration is modelled as two distinct steps. First the agent leaves the source place (action $\mathbf{LP_A}$) and then arrives at the destination place (action $\mathbf{AP_B}$). Additionally an agent can send messages (action $\mathbf{SM_A}$) and receive messages (action $\mathbf{RM_A}$). These messages are sent to a specific place, i.e. a message can only be received by an agent if sent to the place where this agent is located.

6.2 Agents as Parent Objects

In this section we examine the transformations resulting from the first idea mentioned above, i.e. the use of agents as parent objects. We begin with discussing the idea, and afterwards examine the different transformations of reference counting algorithms in more detail; we first consider the different direct reference counting variants, then weighted reference counting, and finally local reference counting.

We will discuss an optimized variant that combines the *inc* and *dec* message sent to the dependency object γ, for every variant except the weighted reference counting (there no *inc* message is used). In every direct reference counting variant a γ-reference is copied and the number of references is incremented, followed by the deletion of a γ-reference and a decrement of the reference count. By combining the two operations the message complexity is lowered. The local reference counting transformation can be optimized in the same way. While no *inc* and *dec* messages are sent, the associated operations are executed nevertheless on the source place, and can be combined into an update operation.

The disadvantage of this optimization is that the resulting protocol is no longer a direct transformation of the related garbage collection algorithm.

6.2.1 The Idea

We assume that the agent is a parent object. The dependency object γ is referenced by the agent. When an agent terminates, all of its references to dependency objects are deleted. We assume that every agent holds at most one reference to a dependency object. Following the model, whenever an agent migrates, a copy operation is performed for every γ-reference the agent holds.

6.2.2 Simple Reference Counting

Since the migration includes copying of all γ-references, an *inc* message is sent to each dependency object γ (1), which answers with an *ack* message (2), or if the dependency object no longer exists, with a *nack* message. When a *nack* message is received, the respective reference is deleted. Only after receipt of all *ack/nack* messages is the agent allowed to migrate, i.e. this transformation delays the agent migration. The *copy* message is part of the actual migration of the agent (3). The now superfluous γ-reference on S is removed and a *dec* message is sent to the dependency object (4).

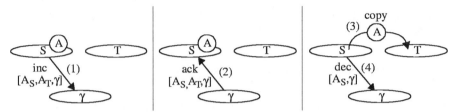

Figure 6-1. Simple reference counting

6.2.2.1 Provided Functionality

In this protocol, an orphan agent is detected directly before it migrates, i.e. when it receives only *nack* messages as answers to the *inc* messages. Thus no orphan agent can migrate.

Finding an agent is only possible, if the *inc* message contains the new location of the agent and if the dependency object stores this information, i.e. the protocol itself does not provide functionality to locate an agent.

6.2.2.2 Protocol

While the copying of a γ-reference is in progress, the participating agents cannot migrate. The variable unBalanced is used to signal whether such an interaction takes place. Thus an agent that wants to migrate has to fulfil the precondition that unBalanced is 0 (action **LP$_S$**). First an <increment γ, LP$_S$, T>-message is sent to every dependency object γ, the variable unBalanced is set to the number of messages sent, and then the agent state is set to the value *inTransit*. As soon as the dependency objects receive this message (action **RLI$_γ$**), it increments its reference count and acknowledges with an <ack γ, LP$_S$, T>-message.

LP$_S$:	[state == alive, unBalanced == 0]
	for all γ-references in dependencySet
	{
	    unBalanced = unBalanced + 1;
	    Send (γ, <increment γ, LP$_S$, T>);
	}
	state = inTransit;

RLI$_γ$:	[a message <increment γ, LP$_S$, T> arrived] Receive (<increment γ, LP$_S$, T>); refCount$_γ$ = refCount$_γ$ + 1; Send (S, <ack γ, LP$_S$, T>);

Algorithm 6-2. Simple reference counting transformed

RLA$_S$:	[state == inTransit, a message <ack γ, LP$_S$, T> arrived]
	Receive (<ack γ, LP$_S$, T>);
	unBalanced = unBalanced - 1;
	if (unBalanced == 0)
	{
	    state = alive;
	    exitPlace();
	    for all γ-references in dependencySet
	    {
	        Send (γ, <decrement γ>);
	    }
	}

AP$_T$:	[state == alive] enterPlace();

Algorithm 6-2. Simple reference counting transformed

Every time one of these <ack γ, LP$_S$, T>-messages is received (action **RLA$_S$**), the variable unBalanced is decremented. When it drops to 0, all dependency objects have acknowledged. Now the state is changed back to alive, the agent leaves the place, and a <decrement γ>-message is sent to every dependency object γ.

6.2.2.3 Optimized Variant

In the optimized variant an *upd* message is sent (1) instead of the original *inc* message. The dependency object γ answers with an *ack* message (2). After receipt of all *ack* messages the agent migrates. The *copy* message is part of the actual migration of the agent (3). The provided functionality is exactly the same as in the unoptimized variant, but now one message less is sent.

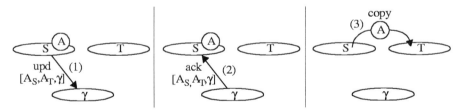

Figure 6-2. Optimized transformation of simple reference counting

6.2.3 The Variant of Lermen and Maurer

Again a migration of an agent includes copying of all of its dependency object references. An *inc* message is sent to every dependency object γ (1), and the copy operation takes place at once in combination with the agent's migration (2). The dependency object γ sends an *ack/nack* message to the target place T. While the first migration is not delayed, all subsequent migrations are delayed until all *ack/nack* messages have been received. After sending both *inc* and *copy* message, the γ-reference is removed from place S, and a *dec* message is sent to the dependency object (4). This protocol variant relies on FIFO communication channels, since without this property the *dec* message could be received before the *inc* message, leading to an unwanted deletion of the dependency object.

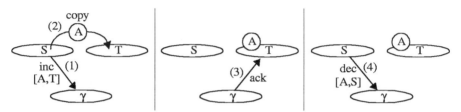

Figure 6-3. Lermen & Maurer variant

6.2.3.1 Provided Functionality

In this protocol, an orphan agent is detected after it has migrated, i.e. when instead of *ack* messages only *nack* messages are sent to the target node. Thus an orphan agent is able to migrate and execute on the target node until all *nack* messages have been received.

This variant also does not provide the functionality to locate an agent. But here the agent's new location has to be sent with the *inc* message, i.e. the only modification to provide such a functionality would be to store the information in the dependency object.

6.2.3.2 Protocol

Since the migration is not delayed in this variant, the agent leaves the source place directly after the <increment γ, LP_S, T>-messages are sent to all dependency objects γ (setting the variable unBalanced to the number of messages sent). After the agent has left the place the respective <decrement γ>-messages are sent to the dependency objects (action **LP_S**). The transformation relies on the FIFO property of the communication channels. Otherwise a <decrement γ>-message might be delivered faster than the <increment γ, LP_S, T>-message, in the worst case leading to the incorrect removal of the dependency object.

As soon as the <increment γ, LP_S, T>-messages are received, the dependency objects increment their reference counts and send an <ack γ, LP_S, T>-message to the target place B (action **$RLI_γ$**). Each time one of these messages is received, unBalanced is decremented (action **RLA_S**). Only after all of the <ack γ, LP_S, T>-messages are received is the agent allowed to migrate again.

LP$_S$:	[state == alive, unBalanced == 0]
	for all γ-references in dependencySet
	{
	    unBalanced = unBalanced + 1;
	    Send (γ, <increment γ, LP$_S$, T>);
	}
	exitPlace();
	for all γ-references in dependencySet
	{
	    Send (γ, <decrement γ>);
	}

RLI$_\gamma$:	[a message <increment γ, LP$_S$, T> arrived] Receive (<increment γ, LP$_S$, T>); refCount$_\gamma$ = refCount$_\gamma$ + 1; Send (T, <ack γ, LP$_S$, T>);
RLA$_T$:	[state == alive, a message <ack γ, LP$_S$, T> arrived] Receive (<ack γ, LP$_S$, T>); unBalanced = unBalanced - 1;
AP$_T$:	[state == alive] enterPlace();

Algorithm 6-3. The Lermen & Maurer variant transformed

6.2.3.3 Optimized Variant

In the optimized variant the original *inc* message is substituted by an *upd* message (1). The copy operation takes place at once in combination with the agent's migration (2). The dependency object γ sends an *ack* message to the target place T. While the first migration is not delayed, all subsequent migrations are delayed until the *ack* messages of all dependency objects have been received. The optimized variant has the same advantages as the unoptimized variant, but additionally the optimization removes the necessity for FIFO communication channels, and one message less is sent. This transformation is essentially the same as the transformation of direct reference counting in Chapter 6.3.2.

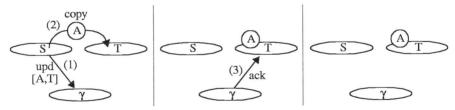

Figure 6-4. Optimized transformation of the Lermen & Maurer variant

6.2.4 The 3-Message Variant of Rudalics

Copying the dependency object references in this variant starts with sending an *inc* message to every dependency object γ (1). Now the agent migrates from place S to place T without copying the γ-references (2). The dependency object γ sends an *copy* message to the agent (3). If the dependency object no longer exists, then a *nack* message is sent instead. After this message is received at T, an *ack/nack* message is sent to place S (4). S now either sends a *dec* message to the dependency object γ, if an *ack* message has been received, or simply deletes the γ-reference if a *nack* message was sent. While the first migration is not delayed, all subsequent migrations are delayed until the *copy* messages have been received and the *ack* messages have been sent. A disadvantage of this protocol variant is the high number of messages.

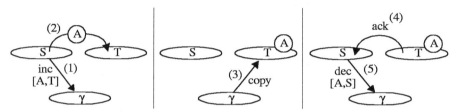

Figure 6-5. Rudalics 3 message variant

6.2.4.1 Provided Functionality

This protocol variant provides the same functionality as the Lermen & Maurer variant. An orphan agent is detected after it has migrated. Thus an orphan agent is able to migrate and execute on the target node until all *nack* messages have been received.

This variant also does not provide the functionality to locate an agent. But here the agent's new location has to be sent with the *inc* message, i.e. the only modification to implement such a functionality would be to store the information in the dependency object.

6.2.4.2 Protocol

Again the migration is not delayed. After sending an <increment γ, LP_S, T>-message to each dependency object (and setting the variable unBalanced), the agent leaves the place (action **LP_S**). As soon as an <increment γ, LP_S, T>-message is received by a dependency object, it increments its reference count and sends a <copy γ, LP_S, T>-message to the target place of the migration (see action **$RLI_γ$**). When this message is received at the target place, the variable unBalanced is decremented and an <ack γ, LP_S, T>-message is sent back to the source place of the migration. The source place, on receiving this message, sends a <decrement γ>-message to the dependency object.

LP$_S$:	[state == alive, unBalanced == 0]
	for all γ-references in dependencySet
	{
	    unBalanced = unBalanced + 1;
	    Send (γ, <increment γ, LP$_S$, T>);
	}
	exitPlace();

RLI$_γ$:	[a message <increment γ, LP$_S$, T> arrived] Receive (<increment γ, LP$_S$, T>); refCount$_γ$ = refCount$_γ$ + 1; Send (T, <copy γ, LP$_S$, T>);
RLC$_T$:	[state == alive, a message <copy γ, LP$_S$, T> arrived] Receive (<copy γ, LP$_S$, T>); unBalanced = unBalanced - 1; Send (S, <ack γ, LP$_S$, T>);
RLA$_S$:	[state == alive, a message <ack γ, LP$_S$, T> arrived] Receive (<ack γ, LP$_S$, T>); Send (γ, <decrement γ>);
AP$_T$:	[state == alive] enterPlace();

Algorithm 6-4. Rudalics 3 message variant transformed

6.2.4.3 Optimized Variant

As above, the *inc* message of the unoptimized variant is replaced by an *upd* message (1). Now the agent migrates from place S to place T without copying the γ-references (2). The dependency object γ sends an *copy* message to the agent (3). If the dependency object no longer exists, then a *nack* message is sent instead. After this message is received at T, an *ack/nack* message is sent to place S (4), and S deletes the γ-reference. The provided functionality is exactly the same as in the unoptimized variant, but now one message less is sent.

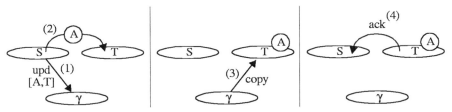

Figure 6-6. Optimized transformation of Rudalics 3-message variant

6.2.5 The 4-Message Variant of Rudalics

The transformed 4 message Rudalics variant is essentially the same as the 3 message variant, with the only difference that the migrating agent contains additional copies of the γ-references.

6.2.6 Weighted Reference Counting

Here the copying of the references implies dividing the reference weight, sending one half with the agent as a copy, and leaving the other half of the reference weight on the place S (1). Normally no contact with the dependency objects is necessary for the copying. Only when the weight is no longer divisible does the dependency object have to be contacted. The reference remaining on S is deleted and a *dec* message containing the reference weight is sent back to the respective dependency objects (2).

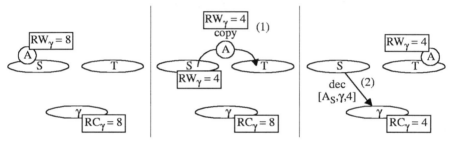

Figure 6-7. Weighted reference counting

6.2.6.1 Provided Functionality

This protocol variant provides an orphan detection functionality comparable to that of the energy concept. The agent receives a reference weight that limits the number of migrations without a contact with the dependency object. On one hand, this minimizes the number of messages needed for the protocol, on the other hand, an orphan is only detected when the weight of the held γ-references is indivisible.

The variant does not provide any functionality to locate an agent. Since the *dec* message can be sent asynchronously, transferring the target location with it would provide only inaccurate information.

6.2.6.2 Protocol

For the sake of simplicity we assume that the respective weights are still divisible. When migrating, the weights of all the dependency object references are halved, <decrement γ, weight$_\gamma$>-messages are sent to the dependency objects, and the agent leaves the place (action **LP$_S$**). In principle dependency object references would have to be installed as well when the weight is divided, only to be removed again when the <decrement γ, weight$_γ$>-messages are sent.

LP$_S$:	[state == alive, unBalanced == 0, all weight$_γ$ are divisible]
	for all γ-references in dependencySet
	{
	    weight$_γ$ = weight$_γ$ / 2;
	    Send (γ, <decrement γ, weight$_γ$>);
	}
	exitPlace();

AP$_T$:	[state == alive] enterPlace();

Algorithm 6-5. Weighted reference counting transformed

6.2.7 Local Reference Counting

In this variant no contact with the dependency objects is necessary on migration. An agent residing on a place has at least one γ-reference. The parent of this reference is the place from which the agent received its dependency object reference (normally the place from which it arrived). When moving from a source place S to a target place T, first a local reference counter for every γ-reference the agent contains is created on S (1). The γ-reference stays on S, and a copy is sent with the agent to the target place S (2), leading to a local reference count of 2 in every installed counter (presuming no other agent already installed local reference counters on this place). When the agent arrives on the target place T, it holds a γ-reference with the source place S as the parent (3). Now the local γ-reference on S is removed, and the local reference

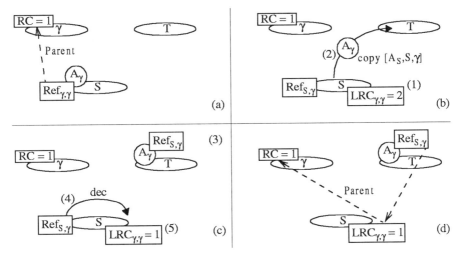

Figure 6-8. Local reference counting

counter on S is decremented (leading to a value of 1). Figure 6-8(a) shows the paternal relationships before the migration and Figure 6-8(d) afterwards.

6.2.7.1 Provided Functionality

Since no contact with the dependency object is initiated, this transformation does not provide any orphan detection functionality. Furthermore, it is not directly usable to locate agents, since the path that is created by the local reference counters points in the wrong direction, i.e. from the agent toward the dependency object γ. In principle the target place and the agent id could be stored in the local reference counter to create a path akin to that of the path concept proposed in Chapter 4.2, with the local reference counter acting as path proxy. But we will see in Chapter 6.3.3 that another transformation leads to the path concept in an even more natural way.

6.2.7.2 Optimized Variant

The optimized variant directly installs the local reference counter with a value of 1 without making a copy of the γ-reference (1), and sends the γ-reference directly with the agent to the source place (2), making a subsequent deletion unnecessary. When the agent arrives on the target place T, it holds a γ-reference with the source place S as the parent (3). Figure 6-9(d) shows the paternal relationship of the different references after the migration. The functionality is exactly the same as in the unoptimized variant. The advantage in comparison to the unoptimized variant is the lower number of operations necessary to implement the protocol.

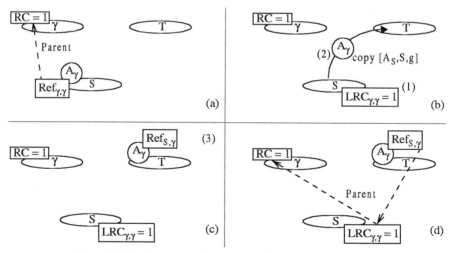

Figure 6-9. *Optimized transformation of local reference counting*

6.2.7.3 Protocol

We choose the optimized variant presented in the previous section for the protocol discussion. When an agent wants to migrate, the different local reference counters have to be installed (if not already an instance exists). If an instance exists, it is incremented. If not, then it is initialized with the value 1 and the parent is set to the parent of the reference held by the agent. After the local reference counter is set, the parent of the reference held by the agent is set to this place, and the agent leaves the place (action **LP$_S$**).

LP$_S$:	[state == alive, unBalanced == 0]
	    for all γ-references in dependencySet
	    {
	        if (place.lrc$_\gamma$!= 0)
	            place.lrc$_\gamma$ = place.lrc$_\gamma$ + 1;
	        else
	        {
	            place.parent$_\gamma$ = parent$_\gamma$;
	            place.lrc$_\gamma$ = 1;
	        }
	        parent$_\gamma$ = place;
	    }
	    exitPlace();

AP$_T$:	[state == alive] enterPlace();

Algorithm 6-6. Local reference counting transformed

6.3 Dependency Objects as Parent Objects

In this section we investigate the transformations resulting from the second idea mentioned above, i.e. defining dependency objects as parent objects. We again start with discussing the idea, and afterwards examine the different transformations in more detail. We first consider direct reference counting, then weighted reference counting and finally local reference counting. We do not consider weighted reference counting, since it leads exactly to the same result as a transformation of direct reference counting.

6.3.1 The Idea

We assume that every dependency object γ is a parent object. A dependency object receives references to every agent that depends on it. It holds references to exactly those agents that depend on it. As soon as the reference count of an agent drops to 0, no dependency object still holds a reference to it; hence it is an orphan, and can be removed.

6.3.2 Direct Reference Counting

As has been said above, all direct reference counting algorithms and the weighted reference counting algorithm yield exactly the same transformation. Here we model migration as follows: an agent that wants to migrate sends a *migration* message to all of its dependency objects (1). The dependency objects delete their references and send *dec* messages to the agent. If a dependency object no longer exists, a *nack* message is sent instead. If a *nack* message is received, the reference count is decremented. As soon as the agent has received all *dec* messages (2), it sets its *migration* flag (MG) and migrates (3). Arrived at the target place, it sends *arrived* messages to the dependency objects (4), and waits for the *ack* (or *nack*) messages to arrive (5). For every received *ack* message it increments its reference count. After all requests have been answered, the *migration* flag is cleared (6). This transformation is essentially the same as the transformation of the Lermen and Maurer variant in Chapter 6.2.3.3.

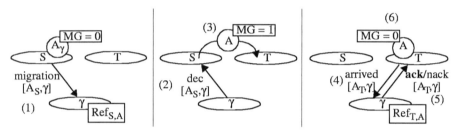

Figure 6-10. Direct reference counting

6.3.2.1 Provided Functionality

In this protocol an orphan is detected directly before migration. If instead of *dec* messages only *nack* messages are received, then the number of references drop to 0, and the agent is recognized as an orphan.

Finding an agent is possible without problems, since the dependency object holds the reference, which includes the location of the agent. On every migration this location is updated. This variant basically implements the same functionality as the agent registration proposed by MASIF and Aglets. One disadvantage is that the update happens before the migration, i.e. the migration is delayed until the *dec* message is received.

6.3.2.2 Direct Reference Counting Optimized

In this optimized variant an *upd* message containing the target place of the agent is sent instead of the original *migration* message (1). The dependency object does not send a *dec* message as in the original transformation, and the agent sets its *migration* flag and migrates at once (2). Instead of sending the *dec* message and waiting for a subsequent *arrived* message from the agent as in the unoptimized variant, the dependency object directly sends an *ack* (or *nack*) message to the target place (3). The agent does not send any *migration* messages; it simply waits for the *ack/nack* messages, and after all of them have arrived, the *migration* flag is cleared (4).

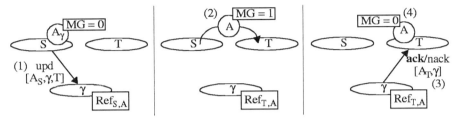

Figure 6-11. Direct reference counting optimized

6.3.2.3 Provided Functionality

The clear advantage of this variant is its lower number of messages. Furthermore the agent is not delayed in its migration. The disadvantage is that now an orphan is only detected at the target site, i.e. an orphan agent is able to migrate and execute on the target node until all *nack* messages have been received.

The functionality to find an agent though is exactly the same as in the unoptimized variant, i.e. this variant also implements the same functionality as the agent registration mechanism.

6.3.2.4 Protocol

We choose the optimized variant presented in the previous section. If an agent wants to migrate, then an <upd γ, T>-message is sent to every dependency object, the variable unBalanced is incremented for every of these messages, and afterwards the agent leaves the place (action **LP$_S$**). When a dependency object receives such an <upd γ, T>-message, it modifies the reference entry of the agent to point to the new location and answers with an <ack γ, upd, T>-message (action **RUD$_γ$**). As soon as this message is received by the agent, it decrements its variable unBalanced (action **RUA$_S$**).

LP$_S$:	[state = alive, unBalanced = 0]
	for all γ-references in dependencySet
	{
	Send (γ, <upd γ, T>);
	unBalanced = unBalanced + 1;
	}
	exitPlace();

Algorithm 6-7. Direct reference counting transformed

RUD_γ:	[a message <upd γ, T> arrived] Receive (<upd γ, T>); dependencySet.modify (S, T); Send (T, <ack γ, upd, S>);
RUA_T:	[state == alive, a message <ack γ, upd, S> arrived] Receive (<ack γ, upd, S>); unBalanced = unBalanced - 1;
AP_T:	[state == alive] enterPlace();

Algorithm 6-7. Direct reference counting transformed

6.3.3 Local Reference Counting

In this variant no contact with the dependency objects is necessary on migration. If an agent wants to migrate from a source place S to a target place T, a reference to A is created (1). This forces the creation of a local reference counter (2). This local reference counter is initialized with the source place as the parent, since the agent is still on the source place. It is set to a value of 2, since 2 copies pointing to this counter exist, the one on the place from which the agent arrived on the source place, and the other the local copy just created. Now the agent is moved to the target place (3) and the parent of the local reference counter on the source place is changed to the target place. The copy made to force the creation of the local reference counter on S is deleted (4) and the counter decremented. Figure 6-12(a) shows the paternal relationships before migration and Figure 6-12(d) afterwards.

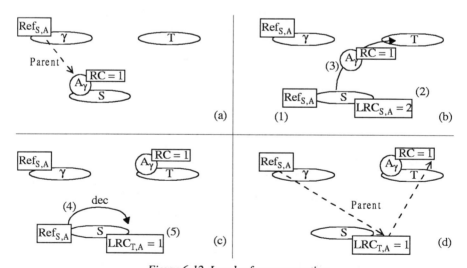

Figure 6-12. Local reference counting

6.3.3.1 Provided Functionality

This transformation provides no orphan detection functionality, since no contact with the dependency object is necessary for the migration.

Finding an agent with this variant is possible without further manipulation of the algorithm. By following the local reference counters, that act as proxies, the agent is eventually found. This variant effectively implements the path concept.

6.3.3.2 Local Reference Counting Optimized

In this optimized variant we do not create a local copy of a reference to the agent. Instead, we initialize the local reference counter with the target place as the parent (1). Now the agent is moved to the target place (2) and instantiated there (3). Figure 6-13(a) and Figure 6-13(d) show that the paternal relationships before and after migration are the same as in the unoptimized version.

6.3.3.3 Provided Functionality

The optimized variant provides exactly the same functionality as the unoptimized transformation. The only difference is the lower number of operations necessary for the implementation of the protocol.

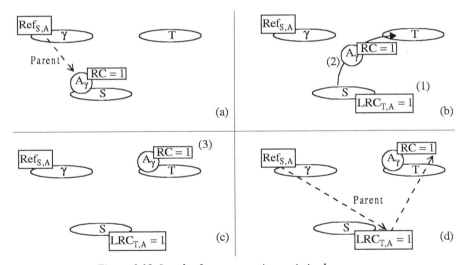

Figure 6-13. Local reference counting optimized

6.3.3.4 Protocol

We choose the optimized variant presented in the last section. Migration in this variant is very simple. First a local reference counter is installed and its parent is set to the target place of the migration (place T). Then the agent leaves the place (action LP_S).

LP_S:	[state == alive, unBalanced == 0]
	place.lrc$_S$ = 1;
	place.parent$_S$ = T;
	exitPlace();

AP_T:	[state == alive] enterPlace();

Algorithm 6-8. Local reference counting transformed

6.4 Assessing the Transformations

For our further considerations we have to choose from the transformations those best suited for control mechanisms. Our requirements (in the order of importance) are:

- the transformation should implement at least one control functionality, i.e. either orphan detection or functionality to find an agent.
- the transformation uses a low number of messages.
- migration of an agent is not delayed. At least the first migration should not be delayed by the protocol.

We will now examine how the presented transformations fulfil the requirements.

6.4.1 Agents as Parent Objects

The message volume is lowest with the transformations of indirect reference counting schemes. But a problem exists, namely that neither information about the migration is conveyed to the dependency object nor a path of proxies is created, i.e. locating an agent is impossible with these transformations. The advantage of both indirect reference counting transformations though is that the migration is never delayed.

The functionality for orphan detection is provided by all of the transformations except the local reference counting variant. While the direct reference counting variants provide orphan detection either directly before or after the migration, the weighted reference counting transformation actually leads to an implementation of the energy concept, i.e. here a simple transformation already yields a comparable mechanism.

The functionality for locating agents is provided by none of the direct reference counting transformations directly. In every one of them minor modifications would be necessary to add the information about the new location of the agent to one of the messages sent by the protocol. In the Lermen and Maurer variant and in the Rudalics 3 and 4 message variants this information is already sent to the dependency object, since it has to send the *ack* message to the target node. Thus the only change would be to store it there. In the case of the local reference counting variant the change would be to additionally store the target node in the local reference counter.

Only the local reference counting variant provides no control functionality, all other mechanisms provide orphan detection functionality. Table 6-1 gives an overview of the different transformations

Type of Transformation	Additional Messages[a]	Delay	Orphan Detection	Locating Agents
Simple Reference Counting (Chapter 6.2.2)	3	Yes	Before Migration	No[b]
Simple Reference Counting Optimized (Chapter 6.2.2.3)	2	Yes	Before Migration	No[b]
Lermen and Maurer[c] (Chapter 6.2.3)	3	Only subsequent migrations[d]	After Migration	No[b]
Lermen and Maurer[e] Optimized (Chapter 6.2.3.3)	2	Only subsequent migrations[c]	After Migration	No[b]
Rudalics 3 Message Variant (Chapter 6.2.4)	4	Only subsequent migrations[c]	After Migration	No[b]
Rudalics 3 Message Variant Optimized (Chapter 6.2.4.3)	3	Only subsequent migrations[c]	After Migration	No[b]
Rudalics 4 Message Variant (Chapter 6.2.5)	4	Only subsequent migrations[c]	After Migration	No[b]
Weighted Reference Counting (Chapter 6.2.6)	1	Never[f]	Comparable to Energy Concept	No
Local Reference Counting (Chapter 6.2.7) Optimized (Chapter 6.2.7.2)	0	Never	No	No[g]

Table 6-1. Properties of the transformations: agents as parent objects

a. compared to migration only (i.e. messages apart from the migration message itself)
b. yes if the information is added to the message
c. assumes FIFO channels
d. until the *ack* message is sent / received
e. similar to the transformation presented in Chapter 6.3.2.2
f. as long as the weight is divisible
g. yes if information is stored in the local reference counters

For our further considerations we choose the optimized Lermen and Maurer variant, since it has the lowest message overhead of the direct reference counting algorithms, and does not delay the agent in its migration, and the weighted reference counting algorithm, since it already implements a functionality comparable to the energy concept.

6.4.2 Dependency Objects as Parent Objects

Both the optimized direct reference counting transformation and the local reference counting transformation have a low message complexity. The LRC transformation needs 0 messages and never delays an agent migration.

The direct reference counting mechanisms provide functionality for orphan detection, the unoptimized variant before the migration, the optimized variant afterwards. No orphan detection functionality is provided by the local reference counting variant.

All of the mechanisms provide functionality to locate agents directly, i.e. without further modification of the protocol. The direct reference counting variants provide a mechanism similar to the agent registration mechanism proposed by MASIF and Aglets. The local reference counting mechanism is similar to the path concept. It creates a path of local reference counters, that can be used as path proxies leading to the agent.

Type of Transformation	Additional Messages[a]	Delay	Orphan Detection	Locating Agents
Direct Reference Counting (Chapter 6.3.2)	4	Yes	Before Migration	Comparable to Registration
Direct Reference Counting[b] Optimized (Chapter 6.3.2.2)	2	Only subsequent migrations[c]	After Migration	Comparable to Registration
Local Reference Counting (Chapter 6.3.3) Optimized (Chapter 6.3.3.2)	0	Never	No	Comparable to Path Concept

Table 6-2. Properties of the transformations: dependency objects as parent objects

  a. compared to migration only (i.e. messages apart from the migration message itself)
  b. similar to the transformation presented in Chapter 6.2.3.3
  c. until the *ack* message is sent / received

For our further considerations we choose the optimized direct reference counting variant, since it implements the registration mechanism and has a lower message volume than the unoptimized variant, and the local reference counting variant, since it provides the same functionality as the path concept.

6.5 Combining the Transformations

By combining mechanisms with different control functionalities we can now create mechanisms that provide orphan detection as well as functionality for locating agents.

Best suited for combination from the first group are the optimized Lermen & Maurer variant and the weighted reference counting variant. From the second group the unoptimized direct reference counting variant needs too many messages, leaving the optimized variant and the local reference counting variant.

If we combine the different variants, we yield Table 6-3. The number of messages given is the maximum of the number of messages for the respective transformations.

Type of Combination	Additional Messages[a]	Delay	Orphan Detection	Locating Agent
Direct Reference Counting opt. plus Lermen and Maurer opt.	2	only subsequent migrations	After Migration	Comparable to Registration
Direct Reference Counting plus Weighted Reference Counting optimized	2	only subsequent migrations	After Migration	Comparable to Registration
Local Reference Counting plus Lermen and Maurer opt.	2	only subsequent migrations	After Migration	Comparable to Registration
Local Reference Counting plus Weighted Reference Counting	1	Never[b]	Comparable to Energy Concept	Comparable to Path Concept with Path Shortening

Table 6-3. Properties of the combinations

a. compared to migration only (i.e. messages apart from the migration message itself)
b. as long as the weight is divisible

On examining the different combinations in detail, we notice that the combinations using the direct reference counting variant provide exactly the same functionality as the original transformation of the direct reference counting algorithm, i.e. we do not add functionality by combining it with either the Lermen and Maurer variant nor the weighted reference counting transformation. The combination of local reference counting and Lermen and Maurer also yields basically the same result. Thus only the combination of local reference counting and weighted reference counting is of interest. This combination has an additional functionality, namely the path shortening discussed in Chapter 4.2.2.1. We will now examine this combination in detail.

6.5.1 Local Reference Counting plus Weighted Reference Counting

In this combination the migration is initiated by a) dividing the weight of the group object references held by the agent and b) by creating a local reference counter for references to the agent pointing toward the target place of the migration (1). Now the agent migrates, together with copies of the dependency object references it holds (2). The dependency object references on the source place S are no longer needed and are deleted. This leads to *dec* messages from S to the dependency objects (3). Upon receiving this message, each dependency object decrements its reference count by the weight sent in the *dec* message (4). Figure 6-14(a) shows the paternal relationships (of the local reference counters) and the distribution of the reference weights before the migration and Figure 6-14(d) afterwards. The original transformations have been presented in Chapter 6.3.3.2 (local reference counting) and Chapter 6.2.6 (weighted reference counting).

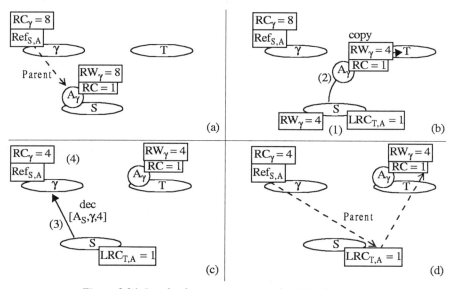

Figure 6-14. Local reference counting and weighted reference counting

6.5.1.1 Provided Functionality

This protocol provides, as the weighted reference counting variant, an orphan detection functionality comparable to the energy concept, limiting the number of migrations of the agent without contact to the dependency object. The drawback is again, that an orphan is only detected when the weight of the held γ-references is indivisible.

Finding an agent with this variant is possible without problems, since the local reference counters effectively act as path proxies pointing toward the agent. A very interesting aspect of this combination is that through the weighted reference counting functionality, effectively, path shortening is implemented for the path created by the local reference counting component.

6.5.1.2 Protocol

For the sake of simplicity we assume that the respective weights are still divisible. When migrating, the weights of all the dependency object references are halved, <decrement γ, weight$_\gamma$>-messages are sent to the dependency objects. Now a local reference counter is installed and its parent is set to the target place of the migration (place T). Then the agent leaves the place (action **LP$_S$**). In principle dependency object references would have to be installed as well when the weight is divided, only to be removed again when the <decrement γ, weight$_\gamma$>-messages are sent, but as in the basic variant, we remove these two operations.

LP$_S$:	[state == alive, unBalanced == 0, all weight$_\gamma$ are divisible]
	for all γ-references in dependencySet
	{
	weight$_\gamma$ = weight$_\gamma$ / 2;
	Send (γ, <decrement γ, weight$_\gamma$>);
	}
	place.lrc$_S$ = 1;
	place.parent$_S$ = T;
	exitPlace();
AP$_T$:	[state == alive]
	enterPlace();

Algorithm 6-9. Combination of WRC and LRC

6.6 Discussion

Let us gather the results of the most interesting transformations in Table 6-4. We see that none of the transformations delays the agent in its migration. The different transformations provide functionality that is comparable to nearly all existing control mechanisms, apart from the advertising and the brute force mechanisms proposed by Aglets and MASIF, and the timed path concept implemented in the shadow concept.

By comparing the different transformations with the mechanisms proposed for the mobile agent paradigm three points are clarified:

- the transformations provide most of the functionality of the control mechanisms for mobile agents, if the different failure model is ignored.
- no timed paths as used in the shadow concept exist in the transformed garbage collection algorithms.
- the transformations bear no new, fundamentally different mechanisms.

Type of Transformation	Additional Messages[a]	Delay	Orphan Detection	Locating Agent
Weighted Reference Counting (Chapter 6.2.6)	1	Never[b]	Comparable to Energy Concept	No
Direct Reference Counting[c] Optimized (Chapter 6.3.2.2)	2	Only subsequent migrations[d]	After Migration	Comparable to Registration
Local Reference Counting (Chapter 6.3.3) Optimized (Chapter 6.3.3.2)	0	Never	No	Comparable to Path Concept
Local Reference Counting plus Weighted Reference Counting	1	Never[b]	Comparable to Energy Concept	Comparable to Path Concept with Path Shortening

Table 6-4. Properties of the useful transformations

a. compared to migration only (i.e. messages apart from the migration message itself)
b. as long as the weight is divisible
c. similar to the transformation presented in Chapter 6.2.3.3
d. until the *ack* message is sent / received

These results show that the set of distributed garbage collection mechanisms corresponds to a subset of mobile agent control mechanisms. It is a true subset, since timed paths as used in the shadow concept, and brute force and advertising as proposed in the MASIF standard, are not found in the transformations. Using the results of TEL AND MATTERN (1993), we can extend this subset relation to the area of termination detection. Thus, if a new, radically different algorithm is developed either in the area of termination detection or in the area of distributed garbage collection, it can be transformed at once and its principles can be exploited for developing new control mechanisms.

There ain't no such thing as a free lunch.

Robert A. Heinlein

7 Comparing the Mechanisms

In Chapter 2, we have discussed the mechanisms for locating mobile agents published by others, and have pointed out their shortcomings. We will now compare these mechanisms with the mechanisms described in this book. We first investigate the functionality provided by the different mechanisms, and categorize them according to the classification given in Chapter 2.5.1. Then we assess them regarding availability, message complexity and consequences for the migration of agents, i.e. the migration delay.

7.1 Functional Comparison

First of all we compare the different mechanisms regarding their functionality and categorize them according to the classification we have provided in Chapter 2.5.1. We distinguish functionality for locating agents and for orphan detection in mobile agent systems. Table 7-1 contains an overview of all those mechanisms that assume a dynamically changing migration path, as has been discussed in Chapter 2.5. None of the mechanisms proposed in MASIF or the Aglets workbench provides orphan detection functionality. The same is true for the path concept and for the local reference counting transformation. All other mechanisms proposed in this book provide orphan detection functionality.

Most of the mechanisms provide functionality for locating agents. The exceptions are advertising, the energy concept and the weighted reference counting transformation. While in the case of the advertising mechanism the success of a search operation depends entirely on the whim of the agent programmer, who decides when / if the agent advertises its current location, in the energy concept and in the weighted reference counting it depends on the consumption of resources, i.e. something the agent is forced to do sooner or later. But essentially these three mechanisms are not suited for locating agents.

Mechanism	Locate Agents	Orphan Detection
Brute force search (MASIF / Aglets)	Yes	No
Registration (MASIF / Aglets)	Yes	No
Logging (MASIF / Aglets)	Yes	No
Advertising (MASIF)	Not guaranteed[a]	No

Table 7-1. Functionality of the different mechanisms

Mechanism	Locate Agents	Orphan Detection
Energy Concept	Eventually[b]	Yes
Paths	Yes	No
Shadows (Basic Mechanism)	Yes	Yes
Weighted Reference Counting (Chapter 6.2.6)	Eventually[b]	Yes
Direct Reference Counting Optimized (Chapter 6.3.2.2)	Yes	Yes
Local Reference Counting Optimized (Chapter 6.3.3.2)	Yes	No
Local Reference Counting plus Weighted Reference Counting (Chapter 6.5.1)	Yes	Yes

Table 7-1. Functionality of the different mechanisms

a. It cannot be guaranteed that the agent is found at all; the agent programmer has to decide when to advertise the location.
b. no worst-case time bound can be given for locating the agent.

7.2 Categorizing the Mechanisms

We categorize the different mechanisms according to the classification given in Figure 2-2; we concentrate on dynamic paths. A mechanism can be found in more than one category, if it combines several of the classified types (see Figure 7-1).

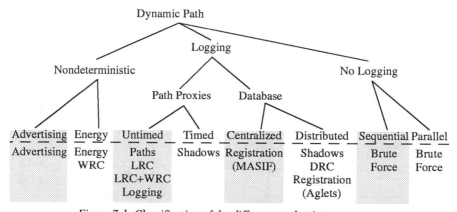

Figure 7-1. Classification of the different mechanisms

It can be seen that the mechanisms developed in Chapter 4 and the combinations from Chapter 6 provide functionality in all classification types apart from advertising and brute force search.

7.3 Assessing the Mechanisms

We start with examining the different mechanisms regarding their functionality and one of the different properties, i.e. availability, message complexity and interference with migration, in turn. Finally, we combine the results of these analyses to assess the mechanisms solely in the light of these three properties.

7.3.1 Availability

We have seen in Chapter 4.3.6, that the limiting availability of mechanisms that rely on an untimed path, i.e. the path concept, logging, LRC, the combination of LRC and WRC, and the hierarchical shadows, is 0. The path is sooner or later no longer usable, and the respective mechanism fails. Hence the availability of these mechanisms is low.

For advertising, energy concept, weighted reference counting, direct reference counting, centralized and distributed database, and for no logging the availability is the same. In every one of these types only the communication channels are involved in the mechanism, which are assumed to have a repair mechanism (see Chapter 4.3.6), i.e. the availability is high. But in the case of energy and advertising type the uncertainty regarding this contact makes these mechanisms unsuited for locating agents.

Timed path proxies have a high availability compared to the untimed path proxies (Chapter 4.3.6 contains the analysis). Thus we yield the results shown in Figure 7-2.

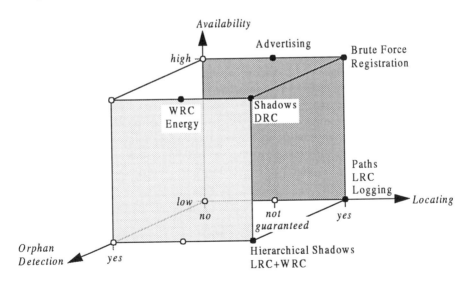

Figure 7-2. *Control mechanisms: functionality vs. availability*

7.3.2 Message Complexity

To allow the comparison of the message complexity of the different mechanisms we define three different degrees: *low*, *medium* and *high* message complexity; we examine the message complexity for maintaining the information and for locating agents. We discuss the respective message complexity for every mechanism in detail in Appendix C. Figure 7-3 shows the different message complexities.

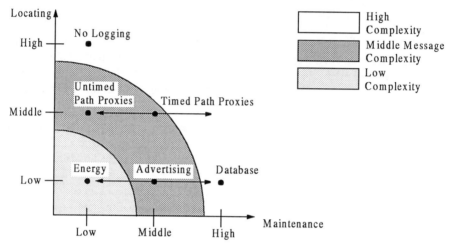

Figure 7-3. The message complexity of the different classified types

Low message overhead for the maintenance is caused by all mechanisms that can be categorized as untimed path proxies, i.e. paths, LRC, LRC+WRC, logging, no logging, and most the non deterministic mechanisms, i.e. energy concept and WRC.

Of medium message complexity for the maintenance are those mechanisms that employ timed path proxies, i.e. the shadow concept, and the advertising mechanism. In the shadow concept additional messages are produced after every time interval to shorten the paths. The exact number of messages depends on this time interval, i.e. the mechanism can be adjusted to different and changing needs. The message complexity for the maintenance of the advertising mechanism solely depends on the programmer and can principally range from low (with inaccurate information) to high, essentially converting the advertising mechanism into a registration mechanism.

A high message volume for the maintenance is created by those mechanisms that update a database for every movement of every agent. These mechanisms are registration, and direct reference counting.

Locating an agent is a different story: here non deterministic mechanisms, i.e. the energy concept, WRC, and advertising have the lowest cost together with the database approaches, i.e. with DRC and with registration.

Medium message complexity for locating agents is created by the untimed or timed path proxies. Here a message must be sent along the path to find the agent.

The highest message volume for locating an agent is produced by the mechanisms classified as no logging, i.e. brute force mechanisms. They produce an extremely high message volume every time an agent is searched. If the sequential variant is used, then the number of messages equals half the number of hosts in the agent system, and in the parallel variant it is the number of hosts (we ignore the message indicating the success).

Since the overall cost can only be given correctly if the application is known exactly, we simplify by defining concentric zones of low, medium and high message complexity (shown in Figure 7-3). Following this classification the energy approach is of low message complexity, advertising, timed path proxies and untimed path proxies are of middle message complexity, and database approaches and approaches using no logging have a high message complexity. Figure 7-4 contains a graphical representation of these results in relation to the functionality provided by the respective mechanism.

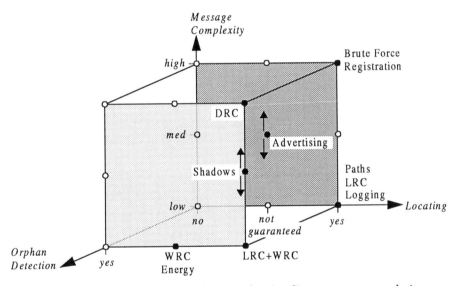

Figure 7-4. Control mechanisms: functionality vs. message complexity

7.3.3 Migration Delay

As we have seen in Chapter 6, three different classes of migration delays exist:
- every migration is delayed; the agent waits for *ack* messages on the source node.
- every but the first migration are delayed; the agent waits for *ack* messages on the target node.
- migrations are never delayed; the agent does not wait for *ack* messages.

Mechanisms of the first class are all those, where a contact is made with a third party before the agent migrates, i.e. the agent is delayed until the answer is received. The second class contains all those mechanisms that contact a third party after the migration takes place, i.e. the agent has to wait for the answer on the target place, and subsequent migrations can only take place after receipt of this answer. The third class of mechanisms never delays the agent, either because no third party is involved, or because no acknowledgment is needed. We name this class *no-delay*. We combine the first and second class and name it *first/following*, since mechanisms of these classes can be transformed into mechanisms of the other class. This is done by sending the acknowledgment to the source place of the migration to convert mechanisms of the second class to mechanisms of the first class, or to the target place to convert mechanisms from the first to second class.

Advertising is in the first/following class, since every time the agent advertises its location it has to wait for the acknowledgment that the information has been received. All those mechanisms updating databases for every migration delay the migration, since the update has to be acknowledged. Thus they are also in the first/following class. The energy concept never delays migration and is thus in the no-delay class. The mechanisms implementing untimed path proxies are in the same no-delay class; they never delay the migration; only a proxy is left on the source place. Timed path proxies also do not delay the migration, i.e. they are also in the no-delay class. Lastly, the brute force mechanism is of the no-delay class, because this mechanism does not modify the migration operation at all. This leads to the results shown in Figure 7-5.

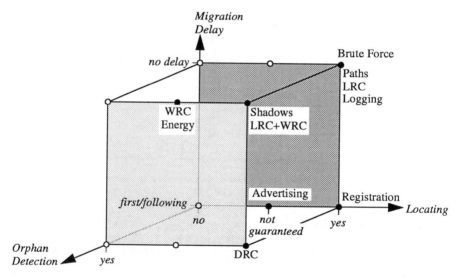

Figure 7-5. Control mechanisms: functionality vs. migration delay

7.3.4 Overall Assessment

If we combine the assessments regarding availability, message complexity and migration delay, we yield Figure 7-6. It can be observed that, apart from the mechanisms implementing untimed paths, i.e. the path concept, LRC, LRC+WRC and logging, all mechanisms show a high availability. But the mechanisms with the lowest message complexity, i.e. advertising, the energy concept and weighted reference counting, are unsuited for locating agents. While the energy type allows orphan detection, the advertising type does not provide this functionality. Thus the advertising type is not usable as a reliable control mechanism for mobile agents.

The mechanism that causes the lowest message overhead while showing a high availability, which is adjustable by changing the *ttl*, is the Shadow concept. This mechanism provides the functionality to locate agents, to detect orphans, and to terminate mobile agents. Furthermore, it does not delay the migration of the mobile agents, i.e. supports best the autonomy of the paradigm.

The mechanisms implementing the database functionality, i.e. registration and the direct reference counting variant, also show high availability, but the message complexity is high and agent migration is delayed. They support only the locating of agents.

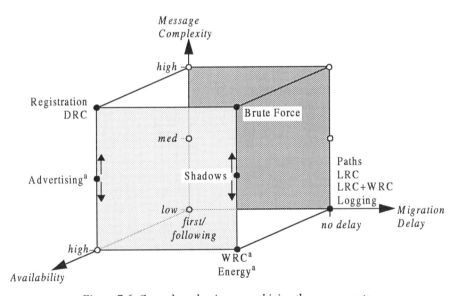

Figure 7-6. Control mechanisms: combining the assessments

a. information provided may be incorrect.

The remaining mechanism for locating agents, brute force, shows high availability while never delaying the migration, but the message complexity is extremely high.

The number of sent messages is at least half the number of hosts in the agent system. This makes the mechanism unusable in a real-world environment.

7.4 Discussion

The results of this chapter are:
- Brute force has an extremely high message complexity compared to all other mechanisms and thus is unusable in real-world mobile agent systems.
- The energy concept and the weighted reference counting transformation are mainly orphan detection mechanisms. They are unsuitable for locating mobile agents.
- The mechanisms using databases exclusively (i.e. registration and the direct reference counting variant) have a high message complexity compared to other mechanisms, i.e. they should not be used as long as alternatives exist. Furthermore, they delay the agent migration, thus interfering with the autonomy of the agent.
- The mechanisms employing the path concept provide only a low availability compared to the other discussed mechanisms. This more than outweighs their advantages of low message complexity and no interference with agent autonomy (i.e. no delay of agent migrations).
- The shadow concept provides functionality for orphan detection and for locating agents. At the same time it has only moderate message complexity compared to most of the other mechanisms to implement the provided functionality with a high availability.
- The shadow concept is the only deterministic mechanisms that allows to adjust message complexity and availability. This is done by changing the allotted time quantum.

The comparison of the different mechanisms yields as a result that the shadow concept provides the best combination of properties (i.e. message complexity, availability and non-interference with the agent autonomy) for the general usage. Furthermore this mechanism provides termination and orphan detection for mobile agents, an additional feature that none of the other mechanisms provides.

The mechanisms provided by MASIF and the Aglets Workbench can still be the better choice for specific applications that provide additional knowledge. In these cases e.g. the advertisement scheme might perform much better by using the application-specific knowledge to decide when to update the location information.

> *The Road goes ever on and on*
> *Down from the door where it began.*
> *Now far ahead the Road has gone,*
> *And I must follow, if I can,*
> *Pursuing it with eager feet,*
> *Until it joins some larger way*
> *Where many paths and errands meet.*
> *And whither then? I cannot say.*
>
> J.R.R. Tolkien, *The Lord of the Rings*

8 Conclusion

Mobile Agents are a promising technology, providing a new viewpoint for implementing applications for distributed systems in widely distributed, heterogeneous open networks. We have seen in Chapter 2 that many applications exist, which, by employing the mobile agent paradigm, show many advantages in coping with today's infrastructure of heterogeneous computers connected by communication systems of varying speed and quality.

For all of these applications, control mechanisms are needed to locate agents, to terminate agents and to detect orphans. Some mechanisms have been published, by MILOJICIC ET AL. (1998) for the MASIF standard, and for the Aglets Workbench by ARIDOR AND OSHIMA (1998), but these mechanisms have shortcomings regarding availability, message complexity and/or the imposed migration delay. Furthermore, none of the mechanisms provides orphan detection functionality.

In this book, we have proposed mechanisms that have a high availability, do not impose a migration delay, and have only low to medium message complexity. The mechanisms provide orphan detection functionality, allow to locate mobile agents, and termination of mobile agents.

We have designed and implemented three mechanisms for the use in mobile agent systems, and examined them regarding their message complexity and availability (in Appendix C). These are the energy concept, the path concept and the shadow concept. In the energy concept an agent gets a certain amount of energy, and if this amount is used up, the agent is terminated. In the path concept, an agent leaves a trail in the system, that can be followed to locate the agent.

The shadow concept combines energy and path concept in a way that leaves the agents most of their autonomy, has low communication costs, and shows a high availability. An agent leaves a trail in the system, but in contrast to the trail in the path concept, this trail is cut short in regular intervals. To allow for simple termination of agents, a delegate of the application is left in the system, the shadow. As long as the shadow exists, all dependent agents are allowed to continue their work. Hence, the agents are no longer depending on the availability of the application instance, i.e. the application may run only intermittently to check for results.

Two variants of the shadow concept have been given, namely hierarchical shadows and mobile shadows. Hierarchical shadows expand the original concept in a way that allows agents as well as applications to create shadows. The mobile shadows variant allows the shadow to move along with the agents to minimize communication costs. Different strategies can be plugged into the shadow, can be combined and can even be changed on the fly to adapt the mechanism to the needs of the agent application.

The examination of the mechanisms regarding availability and message complexity revealed that the path concept has a low message complexity, but shows only a low availability. Both the energy concept and the shadow concept with its variants have a higher message complexity, but at the same time show a much higher availability.

Furthermore, we examined the area of distributed garbage collection for mechanisms suitable for a transformation into control mechanisms for mobile agents. We transformed different reference counting variants, namely simple reference counting, the Lermen & Maurer variant, Rudalics' 3 message and 4 message variant, weighted reference counting and local reference counting. To do this, we introduced dependency objects used in one of the following ways:

- agents are defined as parent objects referencing the dependency object.
- dependency objects are defined as parent objects referencing the agents.

This generic approach covers all possible dependencies between agents and other objects inside the agent system that base on a direct relationship, since the definition of a dependency object in Definition 2-1 explicitly allows a dependency object to be an agent, an object or even a place inside the agent system.

We then examined transformations following the different ideas to combine their functionality. By comparing the transformations with the mechanisms proposed for the mobile agent paradigm the following points have been clarified:

- the transformations provide most of the functionality of the control mechanisms for mobile agents, if the different failure model is ignored.
- no timed paths as used in the shadow concept exist in the transformed garbage collection algorithms.
- the transformations bear no new, fundamentally different mechanisms.

These results show that the set of distributed garbage collection mechanisms corresponds to a subset of mobile agent control mechanisms. It is a true subset, since timed paths as used in the shadow concept are not found in distributed garbage collection. Using the results of TEL AND MATTERN (1993), we can extend this subset relation to the area of termination detection.

Finally, comparing the different mechanisms proposed in here with the mechanisms provided by others, i.e. MASIF and the Aglets Workbench, demonstrated that these mechanisms are superior to the alternatives.

Overall, the different results show the following:
- the existing set of control mechanisms for mobile agents is a superset of the mechanisms that can be derived from distributed garbage collection and termination detection.
- the mechanisms proposed in this book are better than other existing mechanisms in terms of message complexity, migration delay, and availability.

8.1 Future Work

One aspect of every large distributed system has been neglected in all of our discussions, the fact that the costs for messages and the availability of a path along which the messages have to be sent, can vary greatly with the distance between sender and receiver. If, for instance, we assume that a message on a local network costs a hundred times less than on a WAN, and that the local network is a hundred times more reliable than a WAN, then the availability of hierarchical or mobile shadows can look quite different depending on how the shadows and the agents are distributed. By examining the migration sequences of mobile agents in different agent applications it should be possible to derive a model for the distribution of agents in different application classes. By including the different costs the availability and the message complexity for the different mechanisms could be determined with much more precision. This could e.g. lead to a variant of the shadows in which only the needed availability is given as parameter. The mechanism itself could then compute the *time to live* needed to show this availability.

Furthermore, it might be very interesting to introduce the concept of timed paths into implementations of distributed garbage collection. The thus modified algorithms would show a higher availability, making them more suitable for large distributed systems.

Finally, more complex types of dependencies would merit further consideration. A more complex type of dependency, in which e.g. an agent depends on the existence of at least three agents out of five, is, while possible, extremely cumbersome to implement. For each possible subgroup of agents an object depending on these agents would have to be introduced. The agent then would have to depend on these objects representing each subgroup. Better ways to implement these dependencies have been proposed e.g. in BAUMANN AND RADOUNIKLIS (1997) and in PAULUS (1998), but they should be investigated further.

A   Fundamentals of Probability Theory

Most of the work evaluating the reliability and the availability of systems has its roots in probability theory. A good if short introduction can be found in BRONSTEIN AND SEMENDJAJEW (1983). Probability theory is useful in all situations in which the outcome of an experiment is not certain, as is the lifetime of a system. This type of experiment is called *random*. The totality of all possible results of the experiment is called the *sample space*, and a subset of this sample space is called an *event*. An example for such an event is "at least one of the dice shows more than three eyes" in a game of dice. The likelihood of the occurrence of one event in relation to all others is the *probability* of the event. The probability for an event e is written as $P(e)$.

To compute the probability for all sample points, we first define a *random variable* X on the sample space:

Definition A-1:   Random Variable

> A random variable X, on a sample space S, is a function that assigns a real number $X(s)$ to each sample point $s \in S$.

This variable models e.g. the length of a leaf taken randomly from a tree, or the number of atoms in a cm^3 of air. In the next step we assign a probability to these values. This is done by using a distribution function:

Definition A-2:   Cumulative Distribution Function or CDF

> The distribution function F of a random variable X is defined to be the function

$$F(x) = P(X < x), x \in \Re . \qquad \text{(Equation A-1)}$$

This means that the value of the CDF at a point x_0 is the probability for the random variable X being lower than x_0. Thus with the help of the CDF the probability for X being in a specific interval is:

$$P(a \leq X < b) = F(b) - F(a) \qquad \text{(Equation A-2)}$$

The CDF has the following characteristic properties:
1. As a probability the values for $F(x)$ lie between 0 and 1.
2. $F(x)$ is a monotonically nondecreasing function, i.e. $x_1 \leq x_2 \Rightarrow F(x_1) \leq F(x_2)$.
3. $\lim_{x \to +\infty} F(x) = 1$ and $\lim_{x \to -\infty} F(x) = 0$.

A variant of random variables are *continuous random variables,* where for every $x \in \Re$, the set $\{s|X(s) < x, s \in S\}$ is an event. These are the most interesting random variables for reliability models; for instance the lifetime of a system is frequently modelled as a continuous random variable. If a random variable is continuous, then the CDF can be obtained as follows:

$$F(x) = \int_{-\infty}^{x} f(t) dt \qquad \text{(Equation A-3)}$$

with $f(t)$ being the probability density function, which is defined in Definition A-3:

Definition A-3: Probability Density Function or PDF
For a continuous random variable X, the function $f(x) = \frac{d(F(x))}{dx}$ is called the probability density function.

The PDF has the following properties:

1. $f(x) \geq 0$ for all x.
2. Following from $\lim_{x \to \infty} F(x) = 1$ the following holds: $\int_{-\infty}^{+\infty} f(x) dx = 1$.

Thus, with the help of Equation A-2 and Equation A-3 we can define the probability for X being in a specific interval as

$$P(a \leq X < b) = \int_{a}^{b} f(x) dx \qquad \text{(Equation A-4)}$$

For reliability evaluations throughout this thesis we will use an exponential distribution, because it has a very advantageous property called the Markov property. This property implies that if the distribution of an exponentially distributed variable is determined after some time t has elapsed, then after this time the distribution is again exponential. This property models quite well the lifecycle of systems, which, after a burn-in time have a constant reliability for a very long time t in their lifetime until the reliability all of a sudden sinks and the system has to be repaired.

A random variable is exponentially distributed, if the PDF has the following form:

$$f(x) = \begin{cases} \lambda e^{-\lambda x}, & \text{if } 0 \leq x < \infty \\ 0, & \text{otherwise} \end{cases} \qquad \text{(Equation A-5)}$$

We integrate the PDF to obtain the CDF (see Equation A-3) and get:

$$F(x) = \begin{cases} 1-e^{-\lambda x}, & \text{if } 0 \leq x < \infty \\ 0, & \text{otherwise} \end{cases} \qquad \textit{(Equation A-6)}$$

In Figure A-1 exponential probability density functions and exponential cumulative distribution function are shown, with values of 1, 2 and 5 for λ.

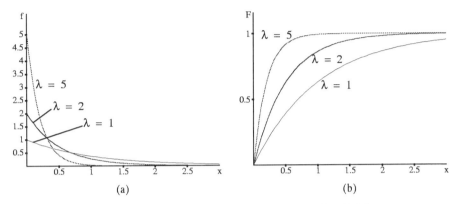

Figure A-1. Exponential distribution of density and probability for $\lambda = 1, 2, 5$. (a) Probability density function f(x). (b) Cumulative distribution function F(x)

Both CDF and PDF completely characterize the behaviour of a random variable. But often such detailed information is not needed; frequently we are interested only in the average, or expectation of a random variable X:

Definition A-4:   Expectation, $E[X]$

The expectation, $E[X]$, of a random variable X is defined by:

$$E[X] = \int_{-\infty}^{+\infty} xf(x)dx \qquad \textit{(Equation A-7)}$$

One example for the expectation is the *mean time to failure* MTTF, which is the expectation of the lifetime of the system.

B   Introduction to Fault Tolerance

B.1   Basic Concepts and Definitions

The most significant attributes of a computer in the context of fault tolerance are *reliability* and *availability*. *Reliability* deals with continuity of service, and *availability* deals with readiness of usage.

B.1.1   Reliability

Let us represent the life of a system, i.e. its time to failure, by a random variable X with a cumulative distribution function F. Then reliability can be defined as follows:

Definition B-1:   Reliability

The reliability of a system is a function $R(t)$ that represents the probability of the system surviving until time t. Thus the reliability is

$$R(t) = P(X > t) = 1 - F(t).\qquad\text{(Equation B-1)}$$

This definition implies that the system is initially working ($R(0) = 1$), and has a finite lifetime ($R(\infty) = 0$).

If F is an exponential distribution over time, then $R(t) = e^{-\lambda t}$. Throughout this book we will assume an exponential distribution for reliability evaluations (see Appendix A for the details). The parameter λ is called the *failure rate*. This leads us to the expected life of the system, or mean time to failure MTTF:

$$\begin{aligned}MTTF &= \int_0^\infty tf(t)\,dt = -\int_0^\infty R'(t)\,dt \\ &= -\int_0^\infty (e^{-\lambda t})'\,dt = \int_0^\infty e^{-\lambda t}\,dt = \frac{1}{\lambda}\end{aligned}\qquad\text{(Equation B-2)}$$

This equation gives the MTTF for a single system. The next problem is to compute the MTTF of a number of connected systems. Two basic ways of connecting systems can be distinguished; either they are used as a series, or in parallel.

Since a series fails if only one of the systems fails, the overall reliability of a series of n systems with exponential distribution function is:

$$R_{Series}(t) = \prod_{i=1}^{n} R_i(t) = \prod_{i=1}^{n} e^{-\lambda_i t} = e^{-t \sum_{i=1}^{n} \lambda_i} \qquad \text{(Equation B-3)}$$

Using Equation B-2 we yield for the MTTF of a series:

$$MTTF_{Series} = \frac{1}{\sum_{i=1}^{n} \lambda_i} \qquad \text{(Equation B-4)}$$

If we assume the same fault rate λ for all parts of the serial system, we yield:

$$MTTF_{Series} = \frac{1}{n\lambda} \qquad \text{(Equation B-5)}$$

This clearly shows that the MTTF of a series is smaller than the MTTF of any one of its systems. If systems are connected in parallel, then the overall reliability is larger than the reliability of a single systems. With exponential distribution, the overall reliability of a parallel system with exponential distribution function is

$$R_{Parallel}(t) = 1 - \prod_{i=1}^{n}(1 - R_i(t)) = 1 - \prod_{i=1}^{n}(1 - e^{-\lambda_i t}) \qquad \text{(Equation B-6)}$$

If we assume the same fault rate λ for all parts of the parallel system, we yield (JALOTE (1994)):

$$MTTF_{Parallel} = \frac{1}{\lambda} \sum_{i=1}^{n} \frac{1}{i}$$

$$\approx \frac{\ln(n)}{\lambda} \qquad \text{(Equation B-7)}$$

B.1.2 Availability

We are not only interested in the mean time until a failure occurs, but also whether a system is alive at a certain time. Thus we define:

Definition B-2: Instantaneous Availability

The instantaneous availability, $A(t)$, of a system is defined as the probability that the system is functioning correctly at time t.

Without repair, this availability is equal to the reliability, i.e. $A(t) = R(t)$. But if a real system fails, then it is repaired or replaced. If we take this into account, then the life of a system can be seen as a sequence of independent random variables representing life and failure. With ANDERSON AND RANDELL (1979) we yield for the instantaneous availability:

$$A(t) = \frac{\mu}{\lambda+\mu} + \frac{\lambda}{\lambda+\mu}e^{-(\lambda+\mu)t}, \text{ with } MTTR = \frac{1}{\mu} \qquad (Equation\ B\text{-}8)$$

In Figure B-1 a graphical representation for the instantaneous availability is given.

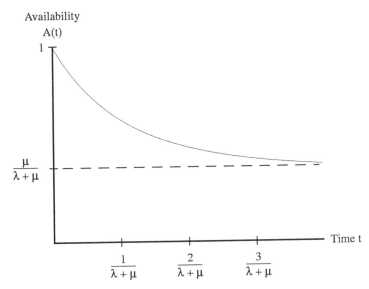

Figure B-1. Availability function for a single component

If we are interested in the availability after a sufficiently long time, then by using the expectations MTTF (mean time to failure) and MTTR (mean time to repair), we can define:

Definition B-3:   Limiting Availability

The limiting availability α is the limit of *A(t)* as *t* approaches infinity.

$$\alpha = \lim_{t \to \infty} A(t) = \frac{MTTF}{MTTF + MTTR} \qquad (Equation\ B\text{-}9)$$

B.2   Failure Classification

A distributed system can be regarded from two different viewpoints: from the viewpoint of the physical components of the system, and from the viewpoint of the computation. The first one is called the *physical model* of the system, the second one the *logical model*. Fault tolerance in distributed systems tries to ensure that the properties, or specified services, of the logical model are preserved in spite of failures in the physical model, i.e. in spite of errors in some of the components in the physical system. Depending on the application area, either the logical model, the physical model or a combination of the models is used as the system model.

But from the user's view it is the logical model that is relevant. Thus a very sensible approach to classify failures in a distributed system is to classify according to the behaviour of a component in the presence of an error, i.e. the type of the failure. This approach specifies the assumptions that can be made if a component fails. The following hierarchic classification is widely used:

- **Crash failure.** If a failure of this type occurs, the component stops at a specific time. With this type of failure, no incorrect state transitions occur when it fails. But it might not be easy for neighbours to detect a failure, because no explicit mechanism to detect it is provided. A variant of this failure type assumes that the components provide a mechanism that allows their neighbours to easily detect the failure. These components, proposed in SCHNEIDER (1984), are called fail-stop processors.
- **Omission failure.** A failure of this type causes a component not to react to some inputs. Two different subtypes of omission failures can be identified, *send omission*, i.e. the faulty process does not send a message which it was supposed to send, and *receive omission*, i.e. the faulty process does not receive a message which it was supposed to receive.
- **Timing failure.** A failure leading a component to react either too early or too late is called a timing failure.
- **Byzantine failure.** Failures in this class cause the components to react in an arbitrary, even malignant manner during the failure.

In this hierarchy of failures the Crash failure is the most restrictive and well-defined type, and the Byzantine failure the least restrictive type. A graphical representation of this hierarchical relationship is depicted in Figure B-2.

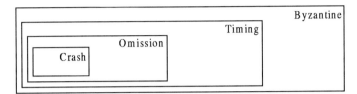

Figure B-2. Failure classification.

JALOTE (1994) defines an additional class, the *incorrect computation failure*, in which an incorrect output is produced. This is clearly a subset of the Byzantine failure, but it is unlike the other failure classes. Typical assumptions for the different components are as follows:

- **Processors:** fail stop, crash failure or Byzantine failure.
- **Communication network:** crash failure, omission failure, timing failure, incorrect computation failure, or Byzantine failure.
- **Clocks:** timing failure or Byzantine failure.
- **Storage Media:** crash failure, timing failure, or Byzantine failure.

C Fault Tolerance and Message Complexity

We now discuss the fault tolerance and the message complexity of the different mechanisms presented in Chapter 4.

C.1 The Energy Concept

C.1.1 Fault Tolerance

In this protocol we have three participants:
- the application node, on which the application, i.e. the dependency object, resides, and from which the agent receives its new energy.
- the agent node, on which the agent resides.
- the communication channel, over which the request and the grant are sent.

We assume that no information is stored on stable storage, i.e. if the application node crashes, then the application is lost, and if the agent node crashes, then the agent is lost.

Since this protocol implements orphan detection, we examine the following: first, whether a failure of the underlying system can incorrectly remove an agent that is no orphan, and second, whether a failure of the underlying system can lead to the continued existence of an orphan agent that should be removed.

Let us first examine, whether the protocol can incorrectly remove an agent in the presence of failures. If the application node crashes, then the application is lost and the agent is an orphan. This will be detected after the agent has consumed its energy. If the agent node crashes, then the agent is lost, and no orphan exists. In both cases the protocol reacts correctly, i.e. is not influenced by the failure. When the communication channel crashes, i.e. if a network partition occurs, then the energy request cannot be delivered, and the agent is removed incorrectly. Thus the protocol depends on the availability of the communication channel to guarantee that no agent is incorrectly recognized as orphan.

Let us now investigate whether every orphan is recognized even in the presence of failures. An agent is an orphan when the dependency object, i.e. in this protocol the application, no longer exists. If the application node crashes before the energy request is received, then no grant is sent back, the agent is correctly recognized as an orphan, and removed. If the communication channel is broken, the same happens. Thus the protocol recognizes every orphan agent correctly.

C.1.2 Message Complexity

The message cost added by the protocol is 2 messages per agent per granted energy request, and 1 additional message for a denied request. If NAK messages are employed, 2 additional messages are needed. If we assume that the common usage of the energy concept is for agents that wait for something, e.g. for a specific change in a remote database, then the request can be piggy-backed on the message signalling the change. This reduces the message cost to 1 message if additional energy is granted and to 0 if denied.

C.2 The Path Concept

C.2.1 Fault Tolerance

In this protocol we have three participants:
- the anchor node, where the agent has been created originally and where the anchor resides.
- the agent node, on which the agent resides.
- the path connecting the anchor node and the agent node, consisting of a number of nodes on which the path proxies are stored and of communication channels between these nodes.

For our discussion we assume a path consisting of n path proxies on n nodes. This will allow us later to compare the availability of the different concepts. These n nodes, the anchor node and the agent node are connected via $n+1$ communication channels. Furthermore, as before, we assume that no information is stored on stable storage, i.e. if the application node crashes, then the application is lost, and if the agent node crashes, then the agent is lost.

Since this protocol implements functionality to locate an agent, we examine the following: first, the availability of the path information stored on the nodes, and second, the availability when we try to follow the path, i.e. when an agent is to be located.

The path information is stored in the respective nodes. Hence we have a series of n nodes for which we compute the availability. Since the proxy information is not stored on stable storage, it is lost after a crash, i.e. we have no repair functionality for the path. Thus the availability $A(t)$ equals the reliability $R(t)$. Let $A_v(t)$ be the availability of a node v. The availability $A_p(t)$ of the path itself, i.e. the availability of the path proxies, can then be calculated by the following equation (see Appendix B.1, Equation B-3):

$$A_p(t) = \prod_{v=1}^{n} A_v(t) \qquad \text{(Equation C-1)}$$

If we simplify the equation by assigning the same availability $A_V(t)$ to every node in the path, then we get the following simple expression:

$$A_p(t) = A_V(t)^n \qquad \text{(Equation C-2)}$$

and since we have no repair functionality, we use Equation B-3 to yield the following result:

$$A_p(t) = e^{-n\lambda_V t} \qquad \text{(Equation C-3)}$$

In Figure C-1 the availability of the path $A_p(t)$ depending on λ and n is shown.

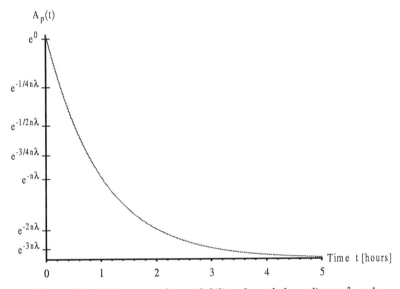

Figure C-1. Path concept: the availability of a path depending on λ and n

It is clear that the limiting availability, being the limit of $A_p(t)$ as t approaches infinity, is 0:

$$\alpha_p = \lim_{t \to \infty} A_p(t) = \lim_{t \to \infty} e^{-n\lambda_V t} = 0 \qquad \text{(Equation C-4)}$$

Let us now examine the availability when we try to follow the path, i.e. for locating an agent. When the protocol tries to locate an agent by following the path, the availability of the communication channels has to be taken into account additionally. Since we have a series of components, i.e. nodes and communication channels, we can compute the availability for searching along the path $A_l(t)$ by multiplying the availability of the nodes, i.e. the availability for the path proxies $A_p(t)$, and the availability of the communication channels $A_c(t)$:

$$A_l(t) = A_p(t)A_c(t) \qquad \text{(Equation C-5)}$$

Let $A_e(t)$ be the availability of a communication channel e. If we assume the same availability $A_E(t)$ for all communication channels, we yield:

$$A_c(t) = A_E(t)^{n+1} \qquad \text{(Equation C-6)}$$

Since we assume that the communication channel is repaired, we use Equation B-8, and yield the following equation for the availability $A_c(t)$ of the communication channels, with λ_E as the failure rate and μ_E as the repair rate of the communication channels:

$$A_c(t) = \left(\frac{\mu_E}{\lambda_E + \mu_E} + \frac{\lambda_E}{\lambda_E + \mu_E} e^{-(\lambda_E + \mu_E)t} \right)^{n+1} \qquad \text{(Equation C-7)}$$

Using this and Equation C-5, we yield for the availability $A_l(t)$ for locating an agent:

$$A_l(t) = e^{-n\lambda_v t} \left(\frac{\mu_E}{\lambda_E + \mu_E} + \frac{\lambda_E}{\lambda_E + \mu_E} e^{-(\lambda_E + \mu_E)t} \right)^{n+1} \qquad \text{(Equation C-8)}$$

The limiting availability for locating an agent α_l is now:

$$\begin{aligned} \alpha_l &= \lim_{t \to \infty} A_l(t) \\ &= \lim_{t \to \infty} e^{-n\lambda_v t} \left(\frac{\mu_E}{\lambda_E + \mu_E} + \frac{\lambda_E}{\lambda_E + \mu_E} e^{-(\lambda_E + \mu_E)t} \right)^{n+1} \end{aligned} \qquad \text{(Equation C-9)}$$

Since the limiting availability for the communication channels α_C is a constant depending on λ_E and μ_E, the limiting availability for locating an agent α_l is 0:

$$\alpha_l = \lim_{t \to \infty} A_l(t) = \alpha_C \lim_{t \to \infty} e^{-n\lambda_v t} = 0 \qquad \text{(Equation C-10)}$$

Thus the path will be broken sooner or later, i.c. it cannot be used to locate an agent, and it cannot be repaired by the protocol. But for short-lived agents the mechanism is usable; this will be discussed in the shadow concept's fault tolerance considerations in Chapter C.3.1.

The first idea that comes to mind to find an agent, if the path is broken, is a broadcast requesting the location of an agent from all places. In Emerald, if the path gets lost, e.g. because a node containing a proxy crashed, a reliable broadcast is used to find the current location of an object (see BLACK ET AL. (1986)). The MASIF proposal and the Aglets system propose a similar mechanism to find agents. But it is obvious that, while in a "small" distributed system such a broadcast might be feasible, in a widely distributed mobile agent system with many participating nodes this approach is not practicable.

C.2.2 Message Complexity

A search request is forwarded along the path, and answered by the agent node sending a message back to the initiator node. If the path contains n proxies, then $n + 1$ messages are sent along the path. Shortening the path involves a message sent from initiator node to anchor node, and sending a "shortenPath" along the old superfluous path. This leads to a cost of $n + 2$ messages for a path length of n, and to $n + 1$ messages if the initiator node is the source node of the last migration, i.e. if the optimization outlined in Chapter 4.2.2.1 is used.

C.3 The Shadow Protocol

C.3.1 Fault Tolerance

As has been said before, the shadow concept is a combination of the energy concept and the path concept, providing both orphan detection for mobile agents and a mechanism for locating agents. In Appendix C.1.1 we have seen that the correctness of the energy concept depends on the availability of the communication channel between the anchor place and the agent place, and in Appendix C.2.1 that the limiting availability for both the path information and the actual locating of an agent is 0, i.e. that no repair functionality is provided by the path concept. We will now compare the different variants of the shadow concept:

- regarding correctness of orphan detection with the energy concept.
- regarding the availability of the path for locating agents with the path concept.

We do not consider the optimizations, because their influence complicates the analysis, and in the worst case the results are the same as the ones presented here, i.e. the same as if the optimizations had not been applied.

C.3.1.1 Basic Protocol

In the basic protocol we have three participants:
- the shadow node, where the shadow resides.
- the agent node, on which the agent resides.
- the path connecting the shadow node and the agent node, consisting of a number of nodes on which the path proxies are stored and of communication channels between these nodes.

We again assume a path consisting of n path proxies on n nodes, to allow the comparison with the path concept. The n nodes, the shadow node and the agent node are connected via $n+1$ communication channels. Furthermore, we again assume that no information is stored on stable storage, i.e. if the shadow node crashes, then the shadow is lost, and if the agent node crashes, then the agent is lost.

Regarding orphan detection we investigate first, whether a failure of the underlying system can incorrectly remove an agent that is no orphan, and second, whether a failure of the underlying system can lead to the continued existence of an orphan agent that should be removed.

Let us first examine, whether the protocol can incorrectly remove an agent in the presence of failures. If the shadow node crashes, then the shadow is lost and the agent is an orphan. This will be detected after the *ttl*. If the agent node crashes, then the agent is lost, and no orphan exists. In both cases the protocol reacts correctly, i.e. is not influenced by the failure. When the communication channel crashes, i.e. if a network partition occurs, then the *ttl* request cannot be delivered, and the agent is removed incorrectly after $ttl + 2(n + 1)d$ (see Figure 4-5). Thus the protocol depends on the availability of the communication channel to guarantee that no agent is incorrectly recognized as orphan. If the communication channel is repaired while the retransmits are in progress, i.e. in the time interval $2(n + 1)d$ after the allotted time quantum has ended, then the protocol recovers. Thus the shadow concept handles short-lived network partitions better than the energy concept, but fails in the same way in the presence of network partitions longer than the time interval $2(n + 1)d$.

Let us now investigate whether every orphan is recognized even in the presence of failures. An agent is an orphan when the dependency object, i.e. the shadow, no longer exists. If the shadow node crashes before the *ttl* request is received, then no grant is sent back, the agent is correctly recognized as an orphan, and removed after the time interval $2(n + 1)d$. If the communication channel crashes, the same happens. Thus the protocol recognizes every orphan agent correctly.

We now examine the availability of the path information, i.e. first, the availability of the path information stored on the nodes, and second, the availability when we try to follow the path, i.e. when an agent is to be located.

As in the path concept, the path information is stored in the respective nodes. Thus we can compute the availability of the path information in the same way. If we assume again that every node in the path has the same availability $A_V(t)$ to every node in the path, we yield:

$$A_p(t) = A_V(t)^n \qquad \text{(Equation C-11)}$$

But in contrast to the path concept, the shadow concept contains a repair functionality for the paths, namely the request for a new *ttl*, in which the shadow is informed about the current location of the agent. By doing this, a new path, unrelated to the old path, is created. Thus every failure in the old path is irrelevant now. The path is, in fact, repaired. The maximum time to repair a broken path is the *ttl* if a failure occurs directly after the new *ttl* has been granted. The minimum time is 0, if a failure occurs just when a new request is sent. Hence the mean time to repair (see Equation B-8) is $ttl/2$. It has to be stressed that this is not the repair time for a specific node or for a specific communication channel, because the whole path is substituted by a new one, but it can be used for computing the path availability in our case. Thus we yield for the instantaneous availability $A_{pn}(t)$ of the path of length n:

$$\begin{aligned}
A_{pn}(t) &= \left(\frac{\mu_V}{\lambda_V + \mu_V} + \frac{\lambda_V}{\lambda_V + \mu_V} e^{-(\lambda_V + \mu_V)t} \right)^n \\
&= \left(\frac{\frac{2}{ttl}}{\lambda_V + \frac{2}{ttl}} + \frac{\lambda_V}{\lambda_V + \frac{2}{ttl}} e^{-\left(\lambda_V + \frac{2}{ttl}\right)t} \right)^n
\end{aligned} \qquad \text{(Equation C-12)}$$

We can already see that the shorter the *ttl* is, the higher the availability becomes. This is reflected in the limiting availability α_{pn}. Using Equation B-5 and Equation B-9, we yield:

$$\alpha_{pn} = \frac{MTTF_p}{MTTF_p + \frac{ttl}{2}} = \frac{\frac{1}{n\lambda_V}}{\frac{1}{n\lambda_V} + \frac{ttl}{2}} = \frac{1}{1 + n\lambda_V \frac{ttl}{2}} \qquad \text{(Equation C-13)}$$

One important point remains to be discussed: until now we have not considered the change in the availability that is induced by the agent migrations and the shortening of the path after the *ttl*. To include this, we have to compute the average of all path lengths between 0 and *n* and use this as the basis for our considerations. Why? When the agent migrates, it increases the path length. Since the path length directly after receiving the *ttl* is 0 (the shadow has to have the current location of the agent), and after the *ttl* is *n*, the agent has to have migrated *n* times, i.e. every path length between 0 and *n* has existed. Thus the instantaneous availability $A_{pn}(t)$ and the limiting availability α_{pn} given above are, in fact, worst-case approximations. The assumption is that the agent, directly after receiving the new time quantum, migrates *n* times and stays on this place until it receives the next time quantum.

Since we do not assume any migration pattern, we approximate the real value by assuming an equal time for every path length, i.e. the agent stays the same time on every place. This leads to the following equation for the availability $A_p(t)$:

$$A_p(t) = \frac{1}{n+1} \sum_{k=0}^{n} \left(\frac{\frac{2}{ttl}}{\lambda_V + \frac{2}{ttl}} + \frac{\lambda_V}{\lambda_V + \frac{2}{ttl}} e^{-\left(\lambda_V + \frac{2}{ttl}\right)t} \right)^k \qquad \text{(Equation C-14)}$$

Using Equation B-5 and Equation B-9, we yield for the limiting availability α_p:

$$\alpha_p = \frac{1}{n+1} \sum_{k=0}^{n} \alpha_{pk} = \frac{1}{n+1} \sum_{k=0}^{n} \frac{1}{1 + k\lambda_V \frac{ttl}{2}} \qquad \text{(Equation C-15)}$$

Let us now examine the availability when we try to follow the path, i.e. for locating an agent. As in the path concept, for following the path the availability of the communication channels has to be taken into account additionally. Since we have a series of components, i.e. nodes and communication channels, we can compute the availability for searching along the path $A_l(t)$ by multiplying the availability of the nodes, i.e. the availability for the path proxies $A_{pn}(t)$, and the availability of the communication channels $A_{cn}(t)$ for every k between 0 and n, and compute the average:

$$A_l(t) = \frac{1}{n+1} \sum_{k=0}^{n} A_{pk}(t) A_{ck}(t) \qquad \text{(Equation C-16)}$$

Let $A_e(t)$ be the availability of a communication channel e. We again assume the same availability $A_E(t)$ for all communication channels. As has been said above, the mean time to repair is now $ttl/2$. We yield the following equation for the availability $A_c(t)$ of the communication channels (with λ_E as the failure rate of the communication channels):

$$A_c(t) = \left(\frac{\frac{2}{ttl}}{\lambda_E + \frac{2}{ttl}} + \frac{\lambda_E}{\lambda_E + \frac{2}{ttl}} e^{-\left(\lambda_E + \frac{2}{ttl}\right)t} \right)^{n+1}$$

(Equation C-17)

Using this and Equation C-16, we yield for the availability $A_l(t)$ for locating an agent:

$$A_l(t) = \frac{1}{n+1} \sum_{k=0}^{n} \left[\left(\frac{\frac{2}{ttl}}{\lambda_V + \frac{2}{ttl}} + \frac{\lambda_V}{\lambda_V + \frac{2}{ttl}} e^{-\left(\lambda_V + \frac{2}{ttl}\right)t} \right)^{k} \right.$$

$$\left. \left(\frac{\frac{2}{ttl}}{\lambda_E + \frac{2}{ttl}} + \frac{\lambda_E}{\lambda_E + \frac{2}{ttl}} e^{-\left(\lambda_E + \frac{2}{ttl}\right)t} \right)^{k+1} \right]$$

(Equation C-18)

We can again see that the shorter the ttl is, the higher the availability becomes. This is reflected in the limiting availability α_l:

$$\alpha_l = \frac{1}{n+1} \sum_{k=0}^{n} \frac{\frac{1}{k\lambda_V + (k+1)\lambda_E}}{\frac{1}{k\lambda_V + (k+1)\lambda_E} + \frac{ttl}{2}}$$

$$= \frac{1}{n+1} \sum_{k=0}^{n} \frac{1}{1 + (k\lambda_V + (k+1)\lambda_E)\frac{ttl}{2}}$$

(Equation C-19)

By adjusting the ttl, we can realize nearly every needed availability. But this holds true only if the lifetime of an agent is longer than the ttl. For an agent lifetime shorter than the ttl, the shadow concept provides exactly the same availability as the path concept, i.e. for short-lived agents the additional protocol overhead of the shadow concept is not necessary.

C.3.1.2   Hierarchical Shadows

In this variant we have the same participants as in the basic protocol, but additionally the nodes on which the hierarchical shadows reside and the communication channels between them are added.

As before, we assume a path connecting agent and hierarchical shadow consisting of n path proxies on n nodes. The n nodes, the shadow node and the agent node are connected via $n+1$ communication channels. We assume n_h hierarchical shadows and n_h+1 communication channels connecting them. Furthermore, we again assume that no information is stored on stable storage, i.e. if the shadow node crashes, then the shadow is lost, and if the agent node crashes, then the agent is lost. As before we assume the same availabilities for all nodes, and the same availabilities for all communication channels.

For orphan detection the same argumentation holds as in the basic protocol. Thus with this variant, as with the basic protocol, every orphan agent and every orphan hierarchical shadow is correctly recognized as an orphan. But the protocol depends on the communication channel's availability between hierarchical shadow and agent, and between hierarchical shadow and parent shadow, to guarantee that no agent respectively hierarchical shadow is incorrectly recognized as orphan. If the communication channel is repaired while the retransmits are in progress, i.e. for the time interval $2(n+1)d$ after the allotted time quantum has ended, then the protocol recovers. Thus the hierarchical shadow concept handles short-lived network partitions in the same way as the basic protocol, but fails in the same way in the presence of network partitions longer than the time interval $2(n+1)d$.

Let us now examine the availability of the path information for the hierarchical shadows. The availability of the path information connecting agent and hierarchical shadow is the same as in the basic protocol given by Equation C-14. But the availability of the shadow hierarchy has to be included in our considerations. Thus we have not only the availability of the path connecting the agent and the hierarchical shadow, but additionally the availability of all nodes on which a parent shadow of the respective hierarchical shadow resides. The problem with the path created by these nodes is the missing repair functionality, i.e. the availability of this path equals the availability in the path concept.

This gives us the following availability for the path information from application shadow to agent:

$$A_p(t) = A_{ph}(t) A_{pa}(t) \qquad \text{(Equation C-20)}$$

with $A_{ph}(t)$ as the availability of the path along the hierarchical shadows, and $A_{pa}(t)$ as the availability of the path connecting shadow and agent. We yield:

$$A_p(t) = e^{-n_h\lambda_h t} \frac{1}{n_a+1} \sum_{k=0}^{n_a} \left(\frac{\frac{2}{ttl}}{\lambda_V + \frac{2}{ttl}} + \frac{\lambda_V}{\lambda_V + \frac{2}{ttl}} e^{-\left(\lambda_V + \frac{2}{ttl}\right)t} \right)^k \quad \text{(Equation C-21)}$$

It is clear that the limiting availability is 0, since the limiting availability of the path along the hierarchical shadows equals 0 (see Equation C-4).

$$\alpha_p = \lim_{t \to \infty} A_p(t)$$

$$= \lim_{t \to \infty} e^{-n_h\lambda_V t} \frac{1}{n_a+1} \sum_{k=0}^{n_a} \left(\frac{\frac{2}{ttl}}{\lambda_V + \frac{2}{ttl}} + \frac{\lambda_V}{\lambda_V + \frac{2}{ttl}} e^{-\left(\lambda_V + \frac{2}{ttl}\right)t} \right)^k$$

$$= 0 \quad \text{(Equation C-22)}$$

To compute the availability for actually following the path, we only have to add the availability of the connecting communication channels a) to the availability of the path along the hierarchical shadows, and b) to the availability of the path connecting the hierarchical shadow and the agent. We yield the following $A_l(t)$:

$$A_l(t) = e^{-n_h\lambda_V t} \left(\frac{\mu_E}{\lambda_E+\mu_E} + \frac{\lambda_E}{\lambda_E+\mu_E} e^{-(\lambda_E+\mu_E)t} \right)^{n_h+1}$$

$$\frac{1}{n_a+1} \sum_{k=0}^{n_a} \left[\left(\frac{\frac{2}{ttl}}{\lambda_V + \frac{2}{ttl}} + \frac{\lambda_V}{\lambda_V + \frac{2}{ttl}} e^{-\left(\lambda_V + \frac{2}{ttl}\right)t} \right)^k \right.$$

$$\left. \left(\frac{\frac{2}{ttl}}{\lambda_E + \frac{2}{ttl}} + \frac{\lambda_E}{\lambda_E + \frac{2}{ttl}} e^{-\left(\lambda_E + \frac{2}{ttl}\right)t} \right)^{k+1} \right] \quad \text{(Equation C-23)}$$

Necessarily, the limiting availability α_l is still 0:

$$\alpha_l = \lim_{t \to \infty} A_l(t) = \lim_{t \to \infty} e^{-n_h\lambda_h t} = 0 \quad \text{(Equation C-24)}$$

C.3.1.3 Mobile Shadows

In this protocol variant we have five participants:
- the shadow home node, where the first shadow proxy is placed.
- the mobile shadow node, where the mobile shadow resides.
- the path connecting the shadow home node and the mobile shadow node, consisting of a number of nodes on which the shadow path proxies are stored and of communication channels between them.
- the agent node, on which the agent resides.
- the path connecting the shadow node and the agent node, consisting of a number of nodes on which the agent path proxies are stored and of communication channels between these nodes.

We assume a path connecting agent and mobile shadow consisting of n_a path proxies on n_a nodes. The n_a nodes, the shadow node and the agent node are connected via n_a+1 communication channels. We assume n_m shadow path proxies and n_m+1 communication channels connecting them. Furthermore, we again assume that no information is stored on stable storage, i.e. if the shadow node crashes, then the shadow is lost, and if the agent node crashes, then the agent is lost. As before we assume the same availabilities for all nodes, and the same availabilities for all communication channels.

For orphan detection the same argumentation holds as in the basic protocol. Thus with this variant, as with the basic protocol, every orphan agent and every orphan mobile shadow is correctly recognized as an orphan. But the protocol depends on the communication channel's availability between mobile shadow and agent, and between mobile shadow and parent shadow, to guarantee that no agent respectively mobile shadow is incorrectly recognized as orphan. If the communication channel is repaired while the retransmits are in progress, i.e. for the time interval $2(n+1)d$ after the allotted time quantum has ended, then the protocol recovers. Thus the mobile shadow concept handles short-lived network partitions in the same way as the basic protocol and the hierarchical shadows, but also fails in the same way in the presence of network partitions longer than the time interval $2(n+1)d$.

Let us now examine the availability of the path information for the mobile shadows. The availability of the path information connecting agent and mobile shadow is the same as in the basic protocol given by Equation C-14. The availability of the path connecting mobile shadow and home shadow proxy is also the same as the availability for the path connecting agent and shadow in the basic protocol given by Equation C-14, albeit with a value of n_m for the path length and a different value for the *ttl*. Thus we have a simple product of the two availabilities:

$$A_p(t) = A_{p_a}(t)^{n_a} A_{p_m}(t)^{n_m} \qquad \textit{(Equation C-25)}$$

As in the basic protocol, the path for the mobile shadows contains a repair functionality for the paths, the request for a new *ttl* for the mobile shadow. Here, as with the agent proxy path, a new path is created, and every failure in the old path is irrelevant. The maximum time to repair a broken path is the *ttl* of the mobile shadow if a failure occurs directly after the shadow's new *ttl* has been granted. The minimum time is 0, if a failure occurs just when a new request is sent. Hence the mean time to repair for the mobile shadow path (see Equation B-8) is $ttl_m/2$. Thus we yield for the instantaneous availability $A_p(t)$ of the path:

$$A_p(t) = \frac{1}{n_a+1} \sum_{k=0}^{n_a} \left(\frac{\mu_{V_a}}{\lambda_V + \mu_{V_a}} + \frac{\lambda_V}{\lambda_V + \mu_{V_a}} e^{-(\lambda_V + \mu_{V_a})t} \right)^k$$

$$\cdot \frac{1}{n_m+1} \sum_{k=0}^{n_m} \left(\frac{\mu_{V_m}}{\lambda_V + \mu_{V_m}} + \frac{\lambda_V}{\lambda_V + \mu_{V_m}} e^{-(\lambda_V + \mu_{V_m})t} \right)^k$$

$$= \frac{1}{n_a+1} \sum_{k=0}^{n_a} \left(\frac{\frac{2}{ttl_a}}{\lambda_V + \frac{2}{ttl_a}} + \frac{\lambda_V}{\lambda_V + \frac{2}{ttl_a}} e^{-\left(\lambda_V + \frac{2}{ttl_a}\right)t} \right)^k$$

$$\cdot \frac{1}{n_m+1} \sum_{k=0}^{n_m} \left(\frac{\frac{2}{ttl_m}}{\lambda_V + \frac{2}{ttl_m}} + \frac{\lambda_V}{\lambda_V + \frac{2}{ttl_m}} e^{-\left(\lambda_V + \frac{2}{ttl_m}\right)t} \right)^k$$

(Equation C-26)

Again we can see that the shorter the respective *ttl* is, the higher the availability becomes. The limiting availability α_p again reflects this:

$$\alpha_p = \sum_{k=0}^{n_a} \frac{MTTF_{pak}}{MTTF_{pak} + \frac{ttl_a}{2}} \cdot \sum_{k=0}^{n_m} \frac{MTTF_{pmk}}{MTTF_{pmk} + \frac{ttl_m}{2}}$$

$$= \sum_{k=0}^{n_a} \frac{1}{1 + k\lambda_V \frac{ttl_a}{2}} \cdot \sum_{k=0}^{n_m} \frac{1}{1 + k\lambda_V \frac{ttl_m}{2}}$$

(Equation C-27)

In contrast to the basic protocol, we now have two paths with different lengths and different *ttl* influencing the availability of the path information. Thus the availability of the path information is lower than the availability of the path information in the basic protocol.

Let us now examine the availability when we try to follow the two paths, i.e. for locating an agent. As before, we have to take the availability of the communication channels into account. We again use $ttl/2$ as the mean time to repair. We now yield for the availability $A_l(t)$ for locating an agent:

$$A_l(t) = \frac{1}{n_a+1} \sum_{k=0}^{n_a} \left[\left(\frac{\frac{2}{ttl_a}}{\lambda_V + \frac{2}{ttl_a}} + \frac{\lambda_V}{\lambda_V + \frac{2}{ttl_a}} e^{-\left(\lambda_V + \frac{2}{ttl_a}\right)t} \right)^k \right.$$

$$\left. \left(\frac{\frac{2}{ttl_a}}{\lambda_E + \frac{2}{ttl_a}} + \frac{\lambda_E}{\lambda_E + \frac{2}{ttl_a}} e^{-\left(\lambda_E + \frac{2}{ttl_a}\right)t} \right)^{k+1} \right]$$

$$\cdot \frac{1}{n_m+1} \sum_{k=0}^{n_m} \left[\left(\frac{\frac{2}{ttl_m}}{\lambda_V + \frac{2}{ttl_m}} + \frac{\lambda_V}{\lambda_V + \frac{2}{ttl_m}} e^{-\left(\lambda_V + \frac{2}{ttl_m}\right)t} \right)^k \right.$$

$$\left. \left(\frac{\frac{2}{ttl_m}}{\lambda_E + \frac{2}{ttl_m}} + \frac{\lambda_E}{\lambda_E + \frac{2}{ttl_m}} e^{-\left(\lambda_E + \frac{2}{ttl_m}\right)t} \right)^{k+1} \right]$$

(Equation C-28)

Here also the respective *ttl* has a high influence on the availability for locating the agent. This is again reflected in the limiting availability α_l:

$$\alpha_l = \frac{1}{n_a+1} \sum_{k=0}^{n_a} \frac{MTTF_{lak}}{MTTF_{lak} + \frac{ttl_a}{2}}$$

$$\cdot \frac{1}{n_m+1} \sum_{k=0}^{n_m} \frac{MTTF_{lmk}}{MTTF_{lmk} + \frac{ttl_m}{2}}$$

(Equation C-29)

By substituting the different MTTFs we yield:

$$\alpha_l = \frac{1}{n_a+1}\sum_{k=0}^{n_a} \frac{\frac{1}{k\lambda_V+(k+1)\lambda_E}}{\frac{1}{k\lambda_V+(k+1)\lambda_E}+\frac{ttl_a}{2}}$$

$$\cdot \frac{1}{n_m+1}\sum_{k=0}^{n_m} \frac{\frac{1}{k\lambda_V+(k+1)\lambda_E}}{\frac{1}{k\lambda_V+(k+1)\lambda_E}+\frac{ttl_m}{2}} \qquad (Equation\ C\text{-}30)$$

$$= \frac{1}{n_a+1}\sum_{k=0}^{n_a} \frac{1}{1+(k\lambda_V+(k+1)\lambda_E)\frac{ttl_a}{2}}$$

$$\cdot \frac{1}{n_m+1}\sum_{k=0}^{n_m} \frac{1}{1+(k\lambda_V+(k+1)\lambda_E)\frac{ttl_m}{2}}$$

By adjusting the respective *ttl*, we can again realize nearly every needed availability. But as before this only holds true if the lifetime of an agent is longer than its *ttl*, and the lifetime of a shadow is longer than its *ttl*, respectively.

C.3.2   Message Complexity

In the following discussion we assume that a proxy path has a length of n, i.e. an agent proxy path has a length of n_a, and a shadow proxy path in the mobile shadows concept a length of n_m.

C.3.2.1   Basic Protocol

Maintaining the Path. As has been described in Chapter 4.3.1 the path is shortened at regular intervals, i.e. every time the agent's *ttl* has dropped to 0. Shortening the path includes one message from agent to shadow (the request) and one from shadow to agent (the grant). The intermediate shadow proxies are removed without additional communication. This leads to a cost of 2 messages per agent per *ttl* request.

Locating Agents. To locate an agent in the basic protocol, a message has to be sent along the proxy path. Thus the message complexity is the same as with the path concept (see Chapter C.2.2), namely $n + 1$ messages along the path, giving a total of $n_a + 1$ messages if the path consists of n_a agent proxies.

Terminating Agents. If the message terminates one agent, then the cost is $n_a + 1$ messages. If all agents a depending on a shadow are terminated, the total costs are $\sum_a (n_a + 1)$ messages.

C.3.2.2 Hierarchical Shadows

Maintaining the Path. Maintaining the path for the agents in the hierarchical shadow protocol has the same complexity as in the basic protocol. But additionally the hierarchical shadows request a new *ttl* at regular, if longer intervals. Thus we have a total cost of 2 messages per agent per ttl_a (the agent's *ttl*) and 2 messages per hierarchical shadow per ttl_h (the hierarchical shadow's *ttl*). With $ttl_h \gg ttl_a$ the cost is approximately the same as in the basic protocol, i.e. 2 messages per agent per ttl_a.

Locating Agents. To locate an agent with the hierarchical shadows, messages have to be sent along the tree of hierarchical shadows. Every shadow sends a message to every child shadow and every child shadow answers with a message as soon as it has received answers from all its children in turn. This leads to 2 messages for every hierarchical shadow, i.e. $2h$ messages with h being the number of hierarchical shadows. These messages are sent regardless of the agent being found. Then the path toward the agent has to be followed, i.e. a message has to be sent along the proxy path, again leading to $n_a + 1$ messages for n_a agent proxies. This leads to a total cost of $2h + n_a + 1$ messages, i.e. substantially higher costs than in the basic protocol.

Terminating Agents. If the message terminates the agent, then no answer from the hierarchical shadows is needed, i.e. 1 message per hierarchical shadow, and following the proxy path is again $n_a + 1$ messages, leading to a total of $h + n_a + 1$ messages. If all agents a depending on a shadow are terminated, the total costs are $h + \sum_a (n_a + 1)$ messages.

C.3.2.3 Mobile Shadows

Maintaining the Path. Again the cost for maintaining the agent paths is the same as in the basic protocol. Maintaining the path for a mobile hierarchical shadow costs the same as the path for a immobile hierarchical shadow, i.e. 2 messages per mobile shadow per ttl_m. Additional costs are produced by the migration of the mobile shadows, which will be regarded as the cost for one additional message. These costs depends on the strategy used for the mobile shadows. In the case of the *Priority-Based* strategy the shadow migrates as often as an agent, in the case of the *Random Agent* strategy the shadow migrates less than once every ttl_a. Thus the resulting cost is 2 messages per agent per ttl_a plus the number of migrations of mobile shadows.

Locating Agents. If mobile shadows are used without hierarchical shadows, then first the shadow proxy path has to be followed, leading to $n_m + 1$ messages for n_m shadow proxies, and afterwards the path of agent proxies, leading to $n_a + 1$ messages for n_a agent proxies. This gives a total of $n_m + n_a + 2$ messages to locate one agent.

If mobile shadows are combined with hierarchical shadows, then as with hierarchical shadows the message is sent to every shadow, but this time along every shadow proxy path of length n_h for every shadow h. The shadows send a message back, and another message is sent along the agent proxy path of length n_a toward the agent. This leads to a cost of $n_a + 3 + \sum_h (n_h + 1)$ messages.

Terminating Agents. If mobile shadows are used without hierarchical shadows, then the costs for terminating one agent are $n_m + n_a + 2$ messages, i.e. $n_m + 1$ messages for following the shadow proxy path, and $n_a + 1$ messages for the agent proxy path. To terminate all agents a depending on a shadow the costs are $n_m + 1 + \sum_a (n_a + 1)$ messages.

Combining mobile shadows with hierarchical shadows again leads to higher costs. To terminate one agent a message has to be sent to every hierarchical shadow along its shadow proxy path consisting of n_h proxies for every shadow h, followed by a message along the agent proxy path of length n_a. This leads to total costs of $n_a + 1 + \sum_h (n_h + 1)$ messages.

To terminate all agents depending on a shadow with combined mobile and hierarchical shadows implies sending a message to every shadow along its shadow proxy path, and to every agent along its agent proxy path. This leads to a cost of $\sum_h (n_h + 1) + \sum_a (n_a + 1)$ messages.

D Bibliography

AGENT SOCIETY (1999)
> The Agent Society (1999), "The Agent society homepage", web page, URL: http://www.agent.org/

ABDULLAHI AND RINGWOOD (1998)
> Abdullahi, S. E. and Ringwood, G. A. (1998), "Garbage collecting the Internet: a survey of distributed garbage collection", *ACM Computing Surveys 30*, 3, pp. 330 - 373.

AGUILERA, CHEN AND TOUEG (1998)
> Aguilera, M. K. and Chen, W. and Toueg, S. (1998), "Failure detection and consensus in the crash-recovery model", Technical Report TR98-1676, Cornell University, Computer Science Department.

ANDERSON AND RANDELL (1979)
> Anderson, T. and Randel, B. (1979), *Computing Systems Reliability*, Cambridge University Press, Cambridge.

APPEL AND HANSON (1988)
> Appel, A. W. and Hanson, D. R. (1988), "Copying garbage collection in the presence of ambigous references", Technical Report CS-TR-162-88, Princeton University, Department of Computing Science.

ARIDOR AND OSHIMA (1998)
> Aridor, Y. and Oshima, M. (1998), "Infrastructure for mobile agents: requirements and design", in *Proceedings of the Second International Workshop on Mobile Agents '98*, K. Rothermel, F. Hohl, Eds., Lecture Notes in Computer Science 1477, Springer-Verlag, Berlin, Germany, pp. 38 - 49.

ARORA, GOUDA AND VARGHESE (1996)
> Arora, A. and Gouda, M. and Varghese, G. (1996), "Constraint satisfaction as a basis for designing nonmasking fault-tolerant systems", *Journal of High Speed Networks 5*, 3, pp. 293 - 306.

AWERBUCH AND PELEG (1995)
> Awerbuch, B. and Peleg, D. (1995), "Concurrent online tracking of mobile users", *Journal of the ACM 42*, 5, pp. 221 - 233

BAL AND TANENBAUM (1990)
> Bal, H. E. and A. S. Tanenbaum, A. S. (1990), "Orca: A language for distributed object-based programming", *SIGPLAN Notes 25*, 5, pp. 17 - 24.

BALDI, GAI AND PICCO (1997)
>Baldi, M. and Gai, S. and Picco, G. (1997), "Exploiting code mobility in decentralized and flexible network management", in *Proceedings of the First International Workshop on Mobile Agents '97*, K. Rothermel, R. Popescu-Celetin, Eds., Lecture Notes in Computer Science 1219, Springer-Verlag, Berlin, Germany, pp. 13 - 26.

BANNAS (1999)
>Horst Bannas (1999), *Personal communication*. Head of the Local Area Network Department, Computer Center, University of Stuttgart.

BAUMANN (1997)
>Baumann, J. (1997), "A protocol for orphan detection and termination in mobile agent systems", Technical Report Nr. 1997/09, Faculty of Computer Science, University of Stuttgart, Germany.

BAUMANN ET AL. (1997)
>Baumann, J. and Hohl, F. and Radouniklis, N. and Rothermel, K. and Straßer, M. (1997), "Communication concepts for mobile agent systems", in *Proceedings of the First International Workshop on Mobile Agents '97*, K. Rothermel, R. Popescu-Celetin, Eds., Lecture Notes in Computer Science 1219, Springer-Verlag, Berlin, Germany, pp. 123 - 135.

BAUMANN AND RADOUNIKLIS (1997)
>Baumann, J. and Radouniklis, N. (1997), "Agent groups for mobile agent systems", in *Distributed Applications and Interoperable Systems*, H. König, K. Geihs and T. Preuß, Eds., Chapman & Hall, London, UK, pp. 74 - 85.

BAUMANN ET AL. (1998A)
>Baumann, J. and Hohl, F. and Rothermel, K. and Straßer, M. (1998), "Mole - concepts of a mobile agent system", *WWW Journal 1*, 3, Baltzer Science Publishers, pp. 123 - 137.

BAUMANN ET AL. (1998B)
>Baumann, J. and Hohl, F. and Rothermel, K. and Schwehm, M. and Straßer, M. (1998), "Mole 3.0: A middleware for java-based mobile software agents", in *Proceedings Middleware '98*, N. Davies, K. Raymond, J. Seitz, Eds., Springer-Verlag London, pp. 355 - 370.

BAUMANN AND ROTHERMEL (1998C)
Baumann, J. and Rothermel, K. (1998), "The Shadow approach: an orphan detection protocol for mobile agents", in *Proceedings of the Second International Workshop on Mobile Agents '98*, K. Rothermel, F. Hohl, Eds., Lecture Notes in Computer Science 1477, Springer-Verlag, Berlin, Germany, pp. 2 - 13, also appeared in *Personal Technologies 2*, 3, Springer-Verlag, London, UK, pp. 100 - 108.

BECK (1997)
Beck, B. (1997), "Terminierung und Waisenerkennung in einem System mobiler Software-Agenten", Diploma Thesis Nr. 1472, Faculty of Computer Science, University of Stuttgart.

BEVAN (1989)
Bevan, D. I. (1989), "An efficient reference counting solution to the distributed garbage collection problem", *Parallel Computing 9*, pp. 179 - 192.

BIRRELL AND NELSON (1984)
Birrell, A. and Nelson, B. (1984), "Implementing remote procedure calls", in *ACM Transactions on Computer Systems 2*, 1, pp. 39 - 59.

BLACK ET AL. (1986)
Black, A. and Hutchinson, N. and Jul, E. and Levy, H. (1986), "Object structure in the Emerald system", in *Proceedings OOPSLA '87*, pp. 78 - 86.

BLACK ET AL. (1987)
Black, A. and Hutchinson, N. and Jul, E. and Levy, H. and Carter, L. (1986), "Distribution and abstract types in Emerald", *IEEE Transactions on Software Engineering 13*, 1, pp. 65 - 76.

BLOOM AND ZDONICK (1987)
Bloom, T. and Zdonick, S. (1987), "Issues in the design of an object-oriented database programming language", in *Proceedings OOPSLA '87*, pp. 441 - 451.

BOEHM (1998)
Boehm, H. J. (1998), "Advantages and disadvantages of conservative garbage collection", web page, URL: http://www.reality.sgi.com/employees/boehm_mti/issues.html.

BRONSTEIN AND SEMENDJAJEW (1983)
Bronstein, I. N. and Semendjajew, K. A. (1983), *Taschenbuch der Mathematik*, Teubner Verlagsgesellschaft, Leipzig, and Verlag Nauka, Moskau.

BRZEZINSKI, HÉLARY AND RAYNAL (1993)
>Brzezinski, J. and Hélary, J. M. and Raynal, M. (1995), "Distributed termination detection: general model and algorithms", in *Proc. 13th IEEE International Conference on Distributed Computing Systems*, IEEE Computer Society Press, pp. 374 - 381.

BUSCHMANN *ET AL.* (1996)
>Buschmann, F. and Meunier, R. and Rohnert, H. and Sommerlad, P. and Stal, M. (1996), *A System of Patterns,* John Wiley & Sons, England.

CARRIERO AND GELERNTER (1989)
>Carriero, N. and Gelernter, D. (1984), "Linda in context", *Communications of the ACM 32*, 4, pp. 444 - 458.

CAUGHEY AND SHRIVASTAVA (1995)
>Caughey, S. J. and Shrivastava, S. K. (1995), "Architectural support for mobile objects in large scale distributed systems", in *Proc. International Workshop on Object Orientation in Operating Systems '95*, IEEE Computer Society Press, also BROADCAST Technical Report Nr. 55.

CARZANIGA *ET AL.* (1997)
>Carzaniga, A. and Picco, G. and Vigna, G. (1997), "Designing distributed applications with mobile code paradigms", in *Proceedings 19th International Conference on Software Engineering*, ACM Press, New York, USA, pp. 22 - 32.

CHADWICK (1994)
>Chadwick, D. (1994), *Understanding the X.500 Directory*, Chapman & Hall, London, UK.

CHANDRASEKARAN AND VENKATESAN (1990)
>Chandrasekaran, S. and Venkatesan, S. (1990), "A message-optimal algorithm for distributed termination detection", *Journal of Parallel and Distributed Computations 8*, pp. 217 - 219.

CHANDY, MISRA AND HAAS (1983)
>Chandy, K. M. and Misra, J. and Haas, L. M. (1983), "Distributed deadlock detection", *ACM Transactions on Computer Systems 1*, pp. 144 - 156.

CHANDY AND LAMPORT (1985)
>Chandy, K. M. and Lamport, L. (1985), "Distributed snapshots: determining global states of distributed systems", *ACM Transactions on Computer Systems 3*, pp. 45 - 56.

CHANDY AND MISRA (1986)
    Chandy, K. M. and Misra, J. (1986), "How processes learn", *Distributed Computing 1*, pp. 40 - 52.

CHANDRA AND TOUEG (1996)
    Chandra, D. T. and Toueg, S. (1996), "Unreliable failure detectors for reliable distributed systems", *Journal of the ACM 43*, 2, pp. 225 - 267.

CHEN AND LENG (1997)
    Chen, W.-S. E. and Leng, C.-W. R. (1997), "A novel mobile agent search algorithm", in *Proceedings of the First International Workshop on Mobile Agents '97*, K. Rothermel, R. Popescu-Celetin, Eds., Lecture Notes in Computer Science 1219, Springer-Verlag, Berlin, Germany, pp. 162 - 173.

CHESS ET AL. (1997)
    Chess, D. and Harrison, C. and Kershenbaum, A. (1997), "Mobile agents: are they a good idea?", in *Mobile Object Systems, Towards the Programmable Internet, Second International Workshop, MO'96, Selected Presentations and Invited Papers*, J. Vitek and C. Tschudin, Eds., Springer, Berlin, Germany, pp. 25-47.

CHIA AND KANNAPAN (1997)
    Chia, T.-H. and Kannapan, S. (1997), "Strategically mobile agents", in *Proceedings of the First International Workshop on Mobile Agents '97*, K. Rothermel, R. Popescu-Celetin, Eds., Lecture Notes in Computer Science 1219, Springer-Verlag, Berlin, Germany, pp. 149 - 161.

COMER AND STEVENS (1993)
    Comer, D. E. and Stevens, D. L. (1993), *Internetworking with TCP-IP: 3rd Volume. Client-server programming and applications*, Prentice-Hall.

CRISTIAN AND FETZER (1998)
    Cristian, F. and Fetzer, C. (1998), "The timed asynchronous distributed system model", in *Proceedings of the Twenty-Eighth Annual International Symposium on Fault-Tolerant Computing*, pp. 140 - 149.

DETLEFS (1990)
    Detlefs, D. L. (1990), "Concurrent, atomic garbage collection", Ph.D. Thesis, Technical Report CMU-CS-90-177, Department of Computer Science, Carnegie Mellon University, USA.

DICKMAN (1996)
>Dickman, P. (1996), "Incremental, distributed orphan detection and actor garbage collection using graph partitioning and Euler cylces", in *Proceedings Workshop on Distributed Algorithms '96*, O. Babaoglu, K. Marzullo, Eds., Lecture Notes in Computer Science 1151, Springer-Verlag, Heidelberg, Germany, pp. 141 - 158.

DIJKSTRA (1975)
>Dijkstra, E. W. (1975), "Guarded commands, nondeterminacy and formal derivation of programs", *Communications of the ACM 18*, 8, pp. 453 - 457.

DIJKSTRA, FEIJEN AND VAN GASTEREN (1983)
>Dijkstra, E. W. and Feijen, W. H. J. and van Gasteren, A. J. M. (1983), "Derivation of a termination detection algorithm for distributed computations", *Information Processing Letters 16 (1983)*, pp. 217-219.

DIJKSTRA AND SCHOLTEN (1980)
>Dijkstra, E. W. and Scholten, C. S. (1980), "Termination detection for diffusing computations", *Information Processing Letters 11 (1989)*, 1, pp. 1 - 4.

DOUGLIS AND OUSTERHOUT (1991)
>Douglis, F. and Ousterhout, J. (1991), "Transparent process migration: design alternatives and the Sprite implementation", in *Software - Practice and Experience 21*, 8, pp. 757 - 785.

DWORK, LYNCH AND STOCKMEYER (1988)
>Dwork, C. and Lynch, N. and Stockmeyer, L. (1988), "Consensus in the presence of partial synchrony", *Journal of the ACM 35*, 2, pp. 288 - 323.

FABIAN (1999)
>Franz Fabian (1999), *Personal communication*. Head of the Computing Laboratory of the Institute of Parallel and Distributed High-Performance Systems, University of Stuttgart.

FALCONE (1987)
>Falcone, J. R. (1987), "A programmable interface language for heterogeneous distributed systems", *ACM Transactions on Computer Systems 5*, 4, pp. 330-351.

FARMER ET AL. (1996)
Farmer, W. and Guttmann, J. and Swarup, V. (1996), "Security for mobile agents: authentication and state appraisal", in *Proceedings of the European Symposium on Research in Computer Security (ESORICS)*, E. Bertino, Ed., Springer-Verlag, Heidelberg, Germany, pp. 118 - 130.

FININ ET AL. (1994)
Finin, T. and Fritzson, R. and McKay, D. and R. McEntire, R. (1994), "KQML as an agent communication language", in *Proceedings of the third Conferenc on Information and Knowledge Management*, ACM Press, pp. 456-463.

FLETCHER AND WATSON (1978)
Fletcher, J. G. and Watson, R. W. (1978), "Mechanisms for a reliable timer-based protocol", in *Computer Network Protocols*, Université de Liège, Belgium, pp. C5-1 - C5-17.

FIPA (1999)
FIPA (1999), "Foundation for Intelligent Physical Agents", web page, URL: http://www.fipa.org/

FOWLER (1985)
Fowler, R. J. (1985), "Decentralized object finding using forwarding addresses", Ph.D. Thesis, Technical Report 85-12-1, Department of Computer Science, University of Washington, USA.

FÜNFROCKEN AND MATTERN (1999)
Fünfrocken, S. and Mattern, F. (1999), "Mobile agents as an architectural concept for Internet-based distributed applications", in *Proceedings KiVS '99, Kommunikation in Verteilten Systemen*, R. Steinmetz, Ed., Informatik aktuell, Springer-Verlag, pp. 32 - 43.

GALLAGER, HUMBLET AND SPIRA (1983)
Gallager, R. G. and Humblet, P. A. and Spira, P. M. (1983), "A distributed algorithm for minimum-weight spanning trees", *ACM Transactions on Programming Languages and Systems 5*, 1, pp. 66 - 77.

GAMMA ET AL. (1994)
Gamma, E. and Helm, R. and Johnson, R. and Vlissides, J. (1994), *Patterns: elements of reusable object-oriented software*, Addison-Wesley, Reading, Massachusetts.

GARCIA-MOLINA ET AL. (1991)
Garcia-Molina, H. and Gawlick, D. and Klein, J. and Kleissner, K. and Salem, K. (1991), "Modeling long-running activities as nested Sagas", *Data Engineering Bulletin 14*, 1, pp. 14 - 18.

GÄRTNER (1998A)
>Gärtner, F. C. (1998), "Fundamentals of fault tolerant distributed computing in asynchronous environments", Technical Report TUD-BS-1998-02, Darmstadt University of Technology, Germany.

GÄRTNER (1998B)
>Gärtner, F. C. (1998), "Specifications for fault tolerance: a comedy of failures", Technical Report TUD-BS-1998-03, Darmstadt University of Technology, Germany.

GENERAL MAGIC (1997)
>General Magic (1997), "Odyssey Web Site", web page, URL: http://www.genmagic.com/agents/

GHEZZI AND VIGNA (1997)
>Ghezzi, C. and G. Vigna, G. (1997),"Mobile code paradigms and technologies: a case study", in *Proceedings of the First International Workshop on Mobile Agents '97*, K. Rothermel, R. Popescu-Celetin, Eds., Lecture Notes in Computer Science 1219, Springer-Verlag, Berlin, Germany, pp. 39 - 49.

GOSCINSKI (1991)
>Goscinski, A. (1991), *Distributed Operating Systems - The Logical Design*, Addison-Wesley, Reading, Massachusetts.

GRAY ET AL. (1996)
>Gray, R. and Cybenko, G. and Kotz, D. and Rus, D. (1996), "Agent Tcl", in *Mobile Agents: Explanations and Examples with CD-ROM*, W. Cockayne and M. Zyda, Eds., Manning Publishing, pp. 58 - 95.

GRAY (1997)
>Gray, R. S. (1997), "AgentTcl: A flexible and secure mobile-agent system", *Dr. Dobbs Journal 22*, 3, San Mateo, USA, pp. 18 - 27.

HAMILTON ET AL. (1998)
>Hamilton, G. and Cattell, R. and Fisher, M. (1998), *JDBC Database Access with Java*, JavaSoft Press, Addison-Wesley, Reading, Massachusetts.

HAMMER AND SHIPMAN (1980)
>Hammer, M. and Shipman, D. (1980), "Reliability mechanisms for SDD-1: a system for distributed databases", in *ACM Transactions on Database Systems 5*, 4, pp. 1 - 17.

HÖFFLINGER (1998)
Höfflinger, J. (1998), "Mobile Shadows: strategies to extend the Shadow protocol for orphan detection and termination in a mobile agent system", Diploma Thesis Nr. 1670, Faculty of Computer Science, University of Stuttgart.

HOHL (1995)
Hohl, F. (1995), "Konzeption eines einfachen Agentensystems und Implementierung eines Prototyps", Diploma Thesis Nr. 1267, Faculty of Computer Science, University of Stuttgart.

HOHL (1997)
Hohl, F. (1997), "An approach to solve the problem of malicious hosts", Technical Report Nr. 1997/03, Faculty of Computer Science, University of Stuttgart.

HOHL, KLAR AND BAUMANN (1997)
Hohl, F. and Klar, P. and Baumann, J. (1997), "Efficient code migration for modular mobile agents", Technical Report Nr. 1997/06, Faculty of Computer Science, University of Stuttgart.

IBM (1997)
IBM Tokyo Research Laboratory (1997), "Aglets-based e-marketplace: concept, architecture and applications", Research Report RT-0253, Tokyo Research Laboratory, Japan.

IBM (1999A)
IBM Corporation (1999), "Messaging and queuing technical reference", web page,
URL: http://www.software.ibm.com/ts/mqseries/

IBM (1999B)
IBM Tokyo Research Laboratory (1999), "Aglets Workbench: programming mobile agents in Java", web page,
URL: http://www.trl.ibm.co.jp/aglets

IBM (1999C)
IBM Tokyo Research Laboratory (1999), "Aglets specification 1.1 draft", web page,
URL: http://www.trl.ibm.co.jp/aglets/spec11.html

ICHISUGI AND YONEZAWA (1990)
Ichisugi, Y. and Yonezawa, A. (1990), "Distributed garbage collection using group reference counting", Technical Report 90-014, Department of Information Science, University of Tokyo, Japan.

IMEX (1999)
> IMEX Research (1999), "1999 High Availability Computing Report", Report, IMEX Research, 1474 Camino Robles, San Jose, CA 95120 USA, executive summary under URL: http://wwww.imexresearch.com/highavailability.html

IONA (1996)
> IONA Technologies Ltd. (1996), "OrbixTalk programming guide", IONA Technologies Inc., Cambridge, MA, USA.

JALOTE (1994)
> P. Jalote (1994), *Fault Tolerance in Distributed Systems*, PTR Prentice Hall.

JAVASOFT (1999)
> JavaSoft, Inc. (1997), "The Java transaction service API", web page, URL: http://java.sun.com/marketing/enterprise/jts.html

JOCHUM (1997)
> Jochum, E. (1997), "Konzeption und Implementierung eines Orphan-Detection Mechanismus nach dem Energiekonzept", Student Thesis Nr. 1642, Faculty of Computer Science, University of Stuttgart.

JOHANSEN ET AL. (1995)
> Johansen, D. and van Renesse, R. and Schneider, F. (1995), "An introduction to the TACOMA distributed system - Version 1.0", Technical Report TR-95-23, University of Tromsø, Tromsø, Norway.

JOHNSON (1994)
> Johnson, D. B. (1994), "Scalable and robust internetwork routing for mobile hosts", *Proceedings of the 14th ICDCS*, IEEE Computer Society, pp. 2 - 11.

JUL ET AL. (1988)
> Jul, E. and Levy, H. and Hutchinson, N. and Black, A. (1988), "Fine-grained mobility in the Emerald system", in *ACM Transactions on Computer Systems 6*, 1, pp. 109 - 133.

KAASHOEK AND TANENBAUM (1991)
> Kaashoek, M. F. and Tanenbaum, A. S. (1991), "Group communication in the Amoeba distributed operating system.", in *Distributed Computing Systems Engineering 1*, 6, pp. 48 - 58.

KAFURA, MUKHERJI AND WASHABAUGH (1995)
Kafura, D. and Mukherji, M. and Washabaugh, D. M. (1995), "Concurrent and distributed garbage collection of active objects", in *IEEE Transactions on Parallel and Distributed Systems 6*, 4, pp. 337 - 350.

KNABE (1995)
Knabe, F. (1995), "Language support for mobile agents", Ph.D. thesis, School of Computer Science, Carnegie Mellon University.

KNAPP (1987)
Knapp, E. (1987), "Deadlock detection in distributed databases", ACM Computing Surveys 19, 4, pp. 303 - 328.

KONSTANTAS ET AL. (1996)
Konstantas, D. and Morin, J. H. and Vitek, J. (1996), "MEDIA: a platform for the commercialization of electronic documents", in *Object Applications*, D. Tsichritzis, Ed., University of Geneva, pp. 7 - 18.

KUBACH (1998)
Kubach, U. (1998), "Multicast-Protokolle und Mobilität im Internet", Diploma Thesis Nr. 1600, Faculty of Computer Science, University of Stuttgart.

LANGE AND OSHIMA (1998)
Lange, D. B. and Oshima, M. (1998), *Programming and Deploying Java Mobile Agents with Aglets*, Addison-Wesley, Reading, Massachusetts.

LANGE AND OSHIMA (1999)
Lange. D. B. and Oshima, M. (1999), "Seven good reasons for mobile agents", *Communications of the ACM 42*, 3, pp. 88 - 89.

LAMPORT (1978)
Lamport, L. (1978), "Time, clocks, and the ordering of events in a distributed system", *Communications of the ACM 21*, 7, pp. 558 - 564.

LERMEN AND MAURER (1986)
Lermen, C. W. and Maurer, D. (1986), "A protocol for distributed reference counting", in *Proc. ACM Conference on Lisp and Functional Programming*, Cambridge, pp. 343 - 354.

LEVY AND TEMPERO (1991)
H. M. Levy, H. M. and E. D. Tempero, E. D. (1991), "Modules, objects and distributed programming issues in RPC and remote object invocation", *Software — Practice & Experience 21*, 1, pp. 77 - 90.

LISKOV (1988)
> Liskov, B. (1988), "Distributed programming in Argus", *Communications of the ACM 31*, 3, 1988.

LYNCH (1996)
> Lynch, N. A. (1996), *Distributed Algorithms*, Morgan Kaufman Publishers Inc., CA, USA.

MANDELBROT (1988)
> Mandelbrot, B. (1988), *Fractal Geometry of Nature*, W. H. Freeman & Co, USA.

MAES (1994)
> Maes, P. (1994), "Agents that reduce work and information overload", *Communications of the ACM 37*, 7, pp. 31 - 40.

MAHESHWARI AND LISKOV (1997)
> Maheshwarei, U. and Liskov, B. (1997), "Collecting cyclic distributed garbage by controlled migration", *Distributed Computing*, 10, pp. 79 - 86.

MATHISKE ET AL. (1997)
> Mathiske, B. and Matthes, F. and Schmidt, J. (1997), "On migrating threads", *Journal of Intelligent Information Systems 8* 2, pp. 167 - 191.

MATTERN (1987A)
> Mattern, F. (1987), "Algorithms for distributed termination detection", *Distributed Computing 2*, pp. 161 - 175.

MATTERN (1987B)
> Mattern, F. (1987), *Verteilte Basisalgorithmen*, Informatik Fachberichte 226, Springer-Verlag, Heidelberg, Germany.

MATTERN (1989)
> Mattern, F. (1989), "Global quiescence detection based on credit distribution and recovery", *Information Processing Letters 30 (1989)*, pp. 195 - 200.

MATTERN ET AL. (1991)
> Mattern, F. and Mehl, H. and Schoone, A. A. and Tel, G. (1991), "Global virtual time approximation with distributed termination algorithms", Technical Report RUU-CS-91-32, Department of Computer Science, University of Utrecht.

MILOJICIC ET AL. (1998)
>Milojicic, D. and Breugst, M. and Busse, I. and Campbell, J. and Covaci, S. and Friedman, B. and Kosaka, K. and Lange, D. and Ono, K. and Oshima, M. and Tham, C. and Virdhagriswaran, S. and White. J. (1998), "MASIF: the OMG mobile agent system interoperability facility", in *Proceedings of the First International Workshop on Mobile Agents '98*, K. Rothermel, F. Hohl, Eds., Lecture Notes in Computer Science 1477, Springer-Verlag, Berlin, Germany, pp. 50 - 67.

MISRA (1983)
>Misra, J. (1983), "Detecting termination of distributed computations using markers" in *Proc. of the second ACM Symposium on Principles of Distributed Computing*, pp. 290 - 294.

MOULY AND PAUTET (1992)
>Mouly, M. and Pautet, M. (1992), *The GSM System for mobile Communication*, Europe Media Publications S. A., ETSI, Palaiseau, France.

MOLE (1999)
>"Mole Project Pages" (1999), University of Stuttgart, web page, URL: http://www.informatik.uni-stuttgart.de/ipvr/vs/projekte/mole.html

MOUNTZIA (1998)
>Mountzia, M. A. (1998), *Flexible Agents in Integrated Network and Systems Management*, Ph.D. thesis, Herbert Utz Verlag, Munich, Germany.

NATARAJAN (1986)
>Natarajan, N. (1986), "A distributed scheme for detecting communication deadlocks", *IEEE Transactions on Software Engineering SE-12*, pp. 531 - 537.

OMG (1994)
>OMG (1994), "Common object services specification", Volume 1, OMG Document Number 94-1-1, Object Management Group, Framingham, MA, USA.

PAULUS (1998)
>Paulus, M. (1998), "Agentengruppen für mobile Agenten", Diploma Thesis Nr. 1664, Faculty of Computer Science, University of Stuttgart.

PANZIERI AND SHRIVASTAVA (1988)
>Panzieri, F. and Shrivastava, S. K. (1988), "Rajdoot: a remote procedure call mechanism supporting orphan detection and killing", *IEEE Transactions on Software Engineering 14*, 1, pp. 30 - 37.

PARRINGTON ET AL. (1995)
>Parrington, G. D. and Shrivastava, S. K. and Wheater, S. M. and Little, M. C. (1995), "The design and implementation of Arjuna", *USENIX Computing Systems Journal 8*, 3, pp. 253 - 306.

PEINE (1996)
>Peine, H. (1996), "Ara: agents for remote action." In *Mobile Agents: Explanations and Examples with CD-ROM*, W. Cockayne, M. Zyda, Eds., Manning Publishing Co., Greenwich, CT, USA, pp. 96 - 164.

PEINE AND STOLPMANN (1997)
>Peine, H. and Stolpmann, T. (1997) "The architecture of the Ara platform for mobile agents", in *Proceedings of the First International Workshop on Mobile Agents '97*, K. Rothermel, R. Popescu-Celetin, Eds., Lecture Notes in Computer Science 1219, Springer-Verlag, Berlin, Germany, pp. 50 - 61.

PIQUER (1991)
>Piquer, J. M. (1991), "Indirect reference counting: a distributed garbage collection algorithm", in *Proc. Parallel Architectures and Languages Europe, Vol. I*, E. H. L. Aarts, J. van Leeuwen, M. Rem, Eds., Lecture Notes in Computer Science 505, Springer-Verlag, pp. 150 - 165.

PIQUER (1996)
>Piquer, J. M. (1996), "Indirect distributed garbage collection: handling object migration", *ACM Transactions on Programming Languages and Systems 18*, 5, pp. 615 - 647.

PLAINFOSSÉ AND SHAPIRO (1995)
>Plainfossé, D. and Shapiro, M. (1995), "A survey of distributed garbage collection techniques", in *Proc. International Workshop on Memory Management*, Kinross, Scotland. pp. 211 - 249.

RAWLINS (1992)
>Rawlins, G. J. E. (1992), *Compared to What? An Introduction to the Analysis of Algorithms*, Computer Science Press, W. H. Freeman and Company, New York, NY10010, USA.

ROTHERMEL *ET AL.* (1997)
Rothermel, K. and Hohl, F. and Radouniklis, N. (1997), "Mobile agent systems: what is missing?", in *Distributed Applications and Interoperable Systems*, H. König, K. Geihs, T. Preuß, Eds., Chapman & Hall, London, UK, pp. 111 - 124.

ROTHERMEL AND SCHWEHM (1998)
Rothermel, K. and Schwehm, M. (1998), "Mobile agents", in *Encyclopedia for Computer Science and Technology*, A. Kent, J. G. Williams, Eds., M. Dekker Inc., New York.

ROTHERMEL AND STRASSER (1998)
Rothermel, K. and Straßer, M. (1998), "A protocol for preserving the exactly-once property of mobile agents", in *Proceedings 17th IEEE Symposium on Reliable Distributed Systems 1998 (SRDS'98)*, IEEE Computer Society, Los Alamitos, California, pp. 100-108.

RUDALICS (1988)
Rudalics, M. (1988), "Multiprocessor list memory management", Ph.D. Thesis, Technical Report RISC-88-87.0, Research Institute for Symbolic Computation, J. Kepler University Linz, Austria.

RUDALICS (1990A)
Rudalics, M. (1990), "Implementation of distributed reference counts", Technical Report RISC-90-39.0, Research Institute for Symbolic Computation, J. Kepler University Linz, Austria.

RUDALICS (1990B)
Rudalics, M. (1990), "Correctness of distributed garbage collection algorithms", Technical Report RISC-90-40.0, Research Institute for Symbolic Computation, J. Kepler University Linz, Austria.

RULIFSON (1969)
Rulifson, J. (1969) "DEL", in *Internet Engineering Task Force, Network Working Group, Request for Comments 5*, ftp://ds.internic.net/rdc/rfc5.txt.

SCHNEIDER (1984)
Schneider, F. B. (1984), "Byzantine generals in action: implementing fail-stop processors", *ACM Transactions on Computer Systems* 2, 2, pp. 145 - 154.

SCHÜTZNER (1999)
Schützner, J. (1999), "Eine Ablaufsteuerung für Workflows mit Mole-Agentengruppen", Student Thesis Nr. 1725, Faculty of Computer Science, University of Stuttgart.

SHAPIRO, DICKMAN AND PLAINFOSSÉ (1992A)
Shapiro, M. and Dickman, P. and Plainfossé, D. (1992), "Robust, distributed references and acyclic garbage collection", in *Proceedings 11th ACM Symposium on Principles of Distributed Computing*, pp. 135 - 146.

SHAPIRO, DICKMAN AND PLAINFOSSÉ (1992B)
Shapiro, M. and Dickman, P. and Plainfossé, D. (1992), "SSP chains: robust, distributed references supporting acyclic garbage collection", Technical Report 1799, INRIA, France.

SHAPIRO ET AL. (1994)
Shapiro, M. and Plainfossé, D. and Ferreira, P. and Amsaleg, L. (1994), "Some key issues in the design of distributed garbage collection and references", in *Unifying Theory and Practice in Distributed Systems*, Dagstuhl, Germany.

SHAVIT AND FRANCEZ (1986)
Shavit, N. and Francez, N. (1986), "A new approach to detection of locally indicative stability", in *Proceedings ICALP '86*, L. Kott, Ed., Lecture Notes in Computer Science 226, Springer-Varlag, pp. 344 - 358.

STAMOS AND GIFFORD (1990)
Stamos, J. W. and Gifford, D. K. (1990), "Remote evaluation", *ACM Transactions on Programmming Languages and Systems 12*, 4, pp. 537 - 565.

STRASSER ET AL. (1996)
Straßer, M. and Baumann, J. and Hohl, F. (1996), "Mole - a Java based mobile agent system", in *Special Issues in Object-Oriented Programming, Workshop Reader of the ECOOP '96*, M. Mühlhäuser, Ed., dpunkt-Verlag, Heidelberg, Germany, pp. 327 - 334.

STRASSER AND SCHWEHM (1997)
Straßer, M. and Schwehm, M. (1997), "A performance model for mobile agent systems", in *Proceedings of the International Conference on Parallel and Distributed Processing Techniques and Applications PDPTA'97, Volume II*, H. R. Arabnia, Ed., Computer Science Research, Education, and Applications Technology (CSREA), pp. 1132 - 1140.

STRASSER, BAUMANN AND SCHWEHM (1999)
　　Straßer, M. and Baumann, J. and Schwehm, M. (1999), "An agent-based framework for the transparent distribution of computations" in *Proceedings 1999 International Conference on Parallel and Distributed Processing Techniques and Applications (PDPTA'99)*, Vol I, CSREA, 1999, pp. 376-382.

STURM (1999)
　　Rick Sturm (1999), "Managing Quality of Service", Summit OnLine Enterprise Management Institute, URL: htttp://www.summitonline.com.

SUN (1994)
　　Sun Microsystems (1994), "The Java language: A white paper", Technical Report, Sun Microsystems, Palo Alto, CA, USA.

SUN (1999)
　　Sun Microsystems (1999), "The Java Web Pages", web page, URL: http://www.javasoft.com

SZASZ (1997)
　　Szasz, V. (1997), "Protokolle zur Synchronisation mobiler Software-Agenten", Student Thesis Nr. 1629, Faculty of Computer Science, University of Stuttgart.

TACOMA (1999)
　　"Tacoma Project Pages" (1999), web page, URL: http://www.cs.uit.no/DOS/Tacoma/index.html

TANENBAUM (1992)
　　Tanenbaum, A. (1992), *Modern Operating Systems*, Prentice Hall.

TANENBAUM (1995)
　　Tanenbaum, A. (1995), *Distributed Operating Systems*, Prentice Hall.

TANENBAUM (1996)
　　Tanenbaum, A. (1996), *Computer Networks*, Third Edition, Prentice Hall.

TEL (1986)
　　Tel, G. (1986), "Distributed infimum approximation", Technical Report RUU-CS-86-12, Department of Computer Science, University of Utrecht.

TEL AND MATTERN (1993)
　　Mattern, F. and Tel, G. (1993), "The derivation of distributed termination detection algorithms from garbage collection schemes", *ACM Transactions on Programming Languages and Systems 15*, 1, pp. 1 - 35.

TEL (1990)

>Tel, G. (1990), "Total algorithms", *Algorithms Review 1*, pp. 13 - 42.

TEL (1994)

>Tel, G. (1994), *Introduction to Distributed Algorithms*. Cambridge University Press.

THEILMANN AND ROTHERMEL (1999)

>Theilmann, W. and Rothermel, K. (1999), "Maintaining specialized search engines through mobile filter agents", in *Proceedings 3rd Int. Workshop on Cooperative Information Agents (CIA'99)*, M. Klusch, O. Shehory, G. Weiß, Eds., Lecture Notes in Artificial Intelligence 1652, Springer, July 1999, pp. 197 - 208.

TSCHUDIN (1993)

>Tschudin, C. F. (1993), "On the structuring of computer communications", Ph.D. Thesis, University of Geneva, Suisse.

USWEST (1999)

>USWest (1999), "Product Description: U S WEST NETWORK 21 Performance Parameters", URL: http://www.uswest.com/products/data/sonet/performance_parameters.html

VIGNA (1997)

>Vigna, G. (1997), "Cryptographic traces for mobile agents", in *Mobile Agents and Security*, G. Vigna, Ed., Lecture Notes in Computer Science 1419, Springer-Verlag, Heidelberg, Germany, pp. 137 - 153.

W3C (1997)

>World Wide Web Consortium (1997), "Jigsaw Overview", web page, URL: http://www.w3.org/Jigsaw/

WALTER (1982)

>Walter, B. (1982), "A robust and efficient protocol for checking the availability of remote sites", in *Proceedings of the 6th Berkeley Workshop on Distributed Data Management and Computer Networks*, Technical Information Department, Lawrence Berkeley Laboratory, University of California, Berkeley, CA, USA, pp. 45 - 67.

WATSON AND WATSON (1987)
    Watson, P. and Watson, I. (1987), "An efficient garbage collection scheme for parallel computer architectures", in *Proceedings Parallel Architectures and Languages Europe, Wol. II*, J. W. de Bakker, A. J. Nijman, P. C. Treleaven, Eds., Lecture Notes in Computer Science 259, Springer-Verlag, pp. 432 - 443.

WHITE (1997)
    White, J. E. (1997), "Telescript", In *Mobile Agents: Explanations and Examples with CD-ROM*, W. Cockayne, M. Zyda, Ed., Manning Publishing, Greenwich, CT, USA, pp. 37 - 57.

WONG *ET AL.* (1997)
    Wong, D. and Paciorek, N. and Walsh, T. (1997), "Concordia: an infrastructure for collaborating mobile agents", in *Proceedings of the First International Workshop on Mobile Agents '97*, K. Rothermel, R. Popescu-Celetin, Eds., Lecture Notes in Computer Science 1219, Springer-Verlag, Berlin, Germany, pp. 86 - 97.

WONG, PACIOREK AND MOORE (1999)
    Wong, D. and Paciorek, N. and Moore, D. (1999), "Java-based mobile agents", *Communications of the ACM 42*, 3, pp. 92 - 102.

ZANDER (1981)
    Zander, J. (1981), "SOFTNET - packet radio in Sweden", in *ARRL Amateur Radio Computer Networking Conferences 1-4*, The American Radio Relay League, Newington, CT, reprinted 1985, pp. 1.7 - 1.10.

ZEPF (1996)
    Zepf, M. (1996), "Entwurf und Implementierung eines einfachen Waisenerkennungsmechanismus für ein Mobile Agenten System", Student Thesis Nr. 1552, Faculty of Computer Science, University of Stuttgart.

ZEPF (1997)
    Zepf, M. (1997), "Modellierung der Abhängigkeiten von Agenten zur Waisenerkennung in einem Mobile-Agenten-System", Diploma Thesis Nr. 1530, Faculty of Computer Science, University of Stuttgart.

Lecture Notes in Computer Science

For information about Vols. 1–1865
please contact your bookseller or Springer-Verlag

Vol. 1866: J. Cussens, A. Frisch (Eds.), Inductive Logic Programming. Proceedings, 2000. X, 265 pages. 2000. (Subseries LNAI).

Vol. 1867: B. Ganter, G.W. Mineau (Eds.), Conceptual Structures: Logical, Linguistic, and Computational Issues. Proceedings, 2000. XI, 569 pages. 2000. (Subseries LNAI).

Vol. 1868: P. Koopman, C. Clack (Eds.), Implementation of Functional Languages. Proceedings, 1999. IX, 199 pages. 2000.

Vol. 1869: M. Aagaard, J. Harrison (Eds.), Theorem Proving in Higher Order Logics. Proceedings, 2000. IX, 535 pages. 2000.

Vol. 1870: P. Deransart, M. Hermenegildo, J. Małuszynski (Eds.), Analysis and Visualization Tools for Constraint Programming. XXI, 363 pages. 2000.

Vol. 1872: J. van Leeuwen, O. Watanabe, M. Hagiya, P.D. Mosses, T. Ito (Eds.), Theoretical Computer Science. Proceedings, 2000. XV, 630 pages. 2000.

Vol. 1873: M. Ibrahim, J. Küng, N. Revell (Eds.), Database and Expert Systems Applications. Proceedings, 2000. XIX, 1005 pages. 2000.

Vol. 1874: Y. Kambayashi, M. Mohania, A M. Tjoa (Eds.), Data Warehousing and Knowledge Discovery. Proceedings, 2000. XII, 438 pages. 2000.

Vol. 1875: K. Bauknecht, S.K. Madria, G. Pernul (Eds.), Electronic Commerce and Web Technologies. Proceedings, 2000. XII, 488 pages. 2000.

Vol. 1876: F. J. Ferri, J.M. Iñesta, A. Amin, P. Pudil (Eds.), Advances in Pattern Recognition. Proceedings, 2000. XVIII, 901 pages. 2000.

Vol. 1877: C. Palamidessi (Ed.), CONCUR 2000 – Concurrency Theory. Proceedings, 2000. XI, 612 pages. 2000.

Vol. 1878: J.P. Bowen, S. Dunne, A. Galloway, S. King (Eds.), ZB 2000: Formal Specification and Development in Z and B. Proceedings, 2000. XIV, 511 pages. 2000.

Vol. 1879: M. Paterson (Ed.), Algorithms – ESA 2000. Proceedings, 2000. IX, 450 pages. 2000.

Vol. 1880: M. Bellare (Ed.), Advances in Cryptology – CRYPTO 2000. Proceedings, 2000. XI, 545 pages. 2000.

Vol. 1881: C. Zhang, V.-W. Soo (Eds.), Design and Applications of Intelligent Agents. Proceedings, 2000. X, 183 pages. 2000. (Subseries LNAI).

Vol. 1882: D. Kotz, F. Mattern (Eds.), Agent Systems, Mobile Agents, and Applications. Proceedings, 2000. XII, 275 pages. 2000.

Vol. 1883: B. Triggs, A. Zisserman, R. Szeliski (Eds.), Vision Algorithms: Theory and Practice. Proceedings, 1999. X, 383 pages. 2000.

Vol. 1884: J. Štuller, J. Pokorný, B. Thalheim, Y. Masunaga (Eds.), Current Issues in Databases and Information Systems. Proceedings, 2000. XIII, 396 pages. 2000.

Vol. 1885: K. Havelund, J. Penix, W. Visser (Eds.), SPIN Model Checking and Software Verification. Proceedings, 2000. X, 343 pages. 2000.

Vol. 1886: R. Mizoguchi, J. Slaney /Eds.), PRICAI 2000: Topics in Artificial Intelligence. Proceedings, 2000. XX, 835 pages. 2000. (Subseries LNAI).

Vol. 1888: G. Sommer, Y.Y. Zeevi (Eds.), Algebraic Frames for the Perception-Action Cycle. Proceedings, 2000. X, 349 pages. 2000.

Vol. 1889: M. Anderson, P. Cheng, V. Haarslev (Eds.), Theory and Application of Diagrams. Proceedings, 2000. XII, 504 pages. 2000. (Subseries LNAI).

Vol. 1890: C Linnhoff-Popien, H.-G. Hegering (Eds.), Trends in Distributed Systems: Towards a Universal Service Market. Proceedings, 2000. XI, 341 pages. 2000.

Vol. 1891: A.L. Oliveira (Ed.), Grammatical Inference: Algorithms and Applications. Proceedings, 2000. VIII, 313 pages. 2000. (Subseries LNAI).

Vol. 1892: P. Brusilovsky, O. Stock, C. Strapparava (Eds.), Adaptive Hypermedia and Adaptive Web-Based Systems. Proceedings, 2000. XIII, 422 pages. 2000.

Vol. 1893: M. Nielsen, B. Rovan (Eds.), Mathematical Foundations of Computer Science 2000. Proceedings, 2000. XIII, 710 pages. 2000.

Vol. 1894: R. Dechter (Ed.), Principles and Practice of Constraint Programming – CP 2000. Proceedings, 2000. XII, 556 pages. 2000.

Vol. 1895: F. Cuppens, Y. Deswarte, D. Gollmann, M. Waidner (Eds.), Computer Security – ESORICS 2000. Proceedings, 2000. X, 325 pages. 2000.

Vol. 1896: R. W. Hartenstein, H. Grünbacher (Eds.), Field-Programmable Logic and Applications. Proceedings, 2000. XVII, 856 pages. 2000.

Vol. 1897: J. Gutknecht, W. Weck (Eds.), Modular Programming Languages. Proceedings, 2000. XII, 299 pages. 2000.

Vol. 1898: E. Blanzieri, L. Portinale (Eds.), Advances in Case-Based Reasoning. Proceedings, 2000. XII, 530 pages. 2000. (Subseries LNAI).

Vol. 1899: H.-H. Nagel, F.J. Perales López (Eds.), Articulated Motion and Deformable Objects. Proceedings, 2000. X, 183 pages. 2000.

Vol. 1900: A. Bode, T. Ludwig, W. Karl, R. Wismüller (Eds.), Euro-Par 2000 Parallel Processing. Proceedings, 2000. XXXV, 1368 pages. 2000.

Vol. 1901: O. Etzion, P. Scheuermann (Eds.), Cooperative Information Systems. Proceedings, 2000. XI, 336 pages. 2000.

Vol. 1902: P. Sojka, I. Kopeček, K. Pala (Eds.), Text, Speech and Dialogue. Proceedings, 2000. XIII, 463 pages. 2000. (Subseries LNAI).

Vol. 1903: S. Reich, K.M. Anderson (Eds.), Open Hypermedia Systems and Structural Computing. Proceedings, 2000. VIII, 187 pages. 2000.

Vol. 1904: S.A. Cerri, D. Dochev (Eds.), Artificial Intelligence: Methodology, Systems, and Applications. Proceedings, 2000. XII, 366 pages. 2000. (Subseries LNAI).

Vol. 1905: H. Scholten, M.J. van Sinderen (Eds.), Interactive Distributed Multimedia Systems and Telecommunication Services. Proceedings, 2000. XI, 306 pages. 2000.

Vol. 1906: A. Porto, G.-C. Roman (Eds.), Coordination Languages and Models. Proceedings, 2000. IX, 353 pages. 2000.

Vol. 1907: H. Debar, L. Mé, S.F. Wu (Eds.), Recent Advances in Intrusion Detection. Proceedings, 2000. X, 227 pages. 2000.

Vol. 1908: J. Dongarra, P. Kacsuk, N. Podhorszki (Eds.), Recent Advances in Parallel Virtual Machine and Message Passing Interface. Proceedings, 2000. XV, 364 pages. 2000.

Vol. 1910: D.A. Zighed, J. Komorowski, J. Żytkow (Eds.), Principles of Data Mining and Knowledge Discovery. Proceedings, 2000. XV, 701 pages. 2000. (Subseries LNAI).

Vol. 1911: D.G. Feitelson, L. Rudolph (Eds.), Job Scheduling Strategies for Parallel Processing. VII, 209 pages. 2000.

Vol. 1912: Y. Gurevich, P.W. Kutter, M. Odersky, L. Thiele (Eds.), Abstract State Machines. Proceedings, 2000. X, 381 pages. 2000.

Vol. 1913: K. Jansen, S. Khuller (Eds.), Approximation Algorithms for Combinatorial Optimization. Proceedings, 2000. IX, 275 pages. 2000.

Vol. 1914: M. Herlihy (Ed.), Distributed Computing. Proceedings, 2000. VIII, 389 pages. 2000.

Vol. 1916: F. Dignum, M. Greaves (Eds.), Issues in Agent Communication. X, 351 pages. 2000. (Subseries LNAI).

Vol. 1917: M. Schoenauer, K. Deb, G. Rudolph, X. Yao, E. Lutton, J.J. Merelo, H.-P. Schwefel (Eds.), Parallel Problem Solving from Nature – PPSN VI. Proceedings, 2000. XXI, 914 pages. 2000.

Vol. 1918: D. Soudris, P. Pirsch, E. Barke (Eds.), Integrated Circuit Design. Proceedings, 2000. XII, 338 pages. 2000.

Vol. 1919: M. Ojeda-Aciego, I.P. de Guzman, G. Brewka, L. Moniz Pereira (Eds.), Logics in Artificial Intelligence. Proceedings, 2000. XI, 407 pages. 2000. (Subseries LNAI).

Vol. 1920: A.H.F. Laender, S.W. Liddle, V.C. Storey (Eds.), Conceptual Modeling – ER 2000. Proceedings, 2000. XV, 588 pages. 2000.

Vol. 1921: S.W. Liddle, H.C. Mayr, B. Thalheim (Eds.), Conceptual Modeling for E-Business and the Web. Proceedings, 2000. X, 179 pages. 2000.

Vol. 1922: J. Crowcroft, J. Roberts, M.I. Smirnov (Eds.), Quality of Future Internet Services. Proceedings, 2000. XI, 368 pages. 2000.

Vol. 1923: J. Borbinha, T. Baker (Eds.), Research and Advanced Technology for Digital Libraries. Proceedings, 2000. XVII, 513 pages. 2000.

Vol. 1924: W. Taha (Ed.), Semantics, Applications, and Implementation of Program Generation. Proceedings, 2000. VIII, 231 pages. 2000.

Vol. 1925: J. Cussens, S. Džeroski (Eds.), Learning Language in Logic. X, 301 pages 2000. (Subseries LNAI).

Vol. 1926: M. Joseph (Ed.), Formal Techniques in Real-Time and Fault-Tolerant Systems. Proceedings, 2000. X, 305 pages. 2000.

Vol. 1927: P. Thomas, H.W. Gellersen, (Eds.), Handheld and Ubiquitous Computing. Proceedings, 2000. X, 249 pages. 2000.

Vol. 1929: R. Laurini (Ed.), Advances in Visual Information Systems. Proceedings, 2000. XII, 542 pages. 2000.

Vol. 1931: E. Horlait (Ed.), Mobile Agents for Telecommunication Applications. Proceedings, 2000. IX, 271 pages. 2000.

Vol. 1658: J. Baumann, Mobile Agents: Control Algorithms. XIX, 161 pages. 2000.

Vol. 1766: M. Jazayeri, R.G.K. Loos, D.R. Musser (Eds.), Generic Programming. Proceedings, 1998. X, 269 pages. 2000.

Vol. 1791: D. Fensel, Problem-Solving Methods. XII, 153 pages. 2000. (Subseries LNAI).

Vol. 1799: K. Czarnecki, U.W. Eisenecker, Generative and Component-Based Software Engineering. Proceedings, 1999. VIII, 225 pages. 2000.

Vol. 1932: Z.W. Raś, S. Ohsuga (Eds.), Foundations of Intelligent Systems. Proceedings, 2000. XII, 646 pages. (Subseries LNAI).

Vol. 1933: R.W. Brause, E. Hanisch (Eds.), Medical Data Analysis. Proceedings, 2000. XI, 316 pages. 2000.

Vol. 1934: J.S. White (Ed.), Envisioning Machine Translation in the Information Future. Proceedings, 2000. XV, 254 pages. 2000. (Subseries LNAI).

Vol. 1935: S.L. Delp, A.M. DiGioia, B. Jaramaz (Eds.), Medical Image Computing and Computer-Assisted Intervention – MICCAI 2000. Proceedings, 2000. XXV, 1250 pages. 2000.

Vol. 1937: R. Dieng, O. Corby (Eds.), Knowledge Engineering and Knowledge Management. Proceedings, 2000. XIII, 457 pages. 2000. (Subseries LNAI).

Vol. 1938: S.Rao, K.I. Sletta (Eds.), Next Generation Networks. Proceedings, 2000. XI, 392 pages. 2000.

Vol. 1939: A. Evans, S. Kent, B. Selic (Eds.), «UML» – The Unified Modeling Language. Proceedings, 2000. XIV, 572 pages. 2000.

Vol. 1940: M. Valero, K. Joe, M. Kitsuregawa, H. Tanaka (Eds.), High Performance Computing. Proceedings, 2000. XV, 595 pages. 2000.

Vol. 1942: K. Masanori, R. Popescu-Zeletin (Eds.), Active Networks. Proceedings, 2000. XI, 424 pages. 2000.

Vol. 1945: W. Grieskamp, T. Santen, B. Stoddart (Eds.), Integrated Formal Methods. Proceedings, 2000. X, 441 pages. 2000.

Vol. 1948: T. Tan, Y. Shi, W. Gao (Eds.), Advances in Multimodal Interfaces – ICMI 2000. Proceedings, 2000. XVI, 678 pages. 2000.